my LiTTLE PONY

CROCHET

Jana Whitley

THUNDER BAY
P · R · E · S · S
SAN DIEGO, CALIFORNIA

Thunder Bay Press

An imprint of Printers Row Publishing Group
10350 Barnes Canyon Road, Suite 100, San Diego, CA 92121
www.thunderbaybooks.com

Thunder Bay Press
Publisher: Peter Norton
Associate Publisher: Ana Parker
Publishing/Editorial Team: April Farr, Kelly Larsen, Kathryn C. Dalby
Editorial Team: JoAnn Padgett, Melinda Allman, Traci Douglas

becker&mayer!
Designer: Scott Richardson
Editor: Meredith Mennitt
Photographer: Chris Burrows
Production Coordinator: Shawn Reed
Product Sourcing: Shawn Reed

Project # 301853

ISBN: 978-1-68412-398-8

Printed and manufactured in Shenzen, China.

22 21 20 19 18   1 2 3 4 5

CONTENTS

Introduction

I am pleased to present this exciting collection of twelve My Little Pony crochet patterns. Each pony figure is about six inches tall and carefully detailed to match the character's colorful signature traits, including embroidered Cutie Marks.

I have arranged the pattern order by their character groups: the Mane 6 and sidekick Spike the Dragon, the princess ponies, then the (formerly) nemesis characters. I hope you will enjoy using the magic of crochet to bring these soft, sweet My Little Pony figures to life. They will keep you company at your desk, brighten up a bookshelf, or make super cute gifts for your pony friends. Wherever these little ponies may roam, they're sure to bring squeals of delight.

Happy crocheting!

—Jana

Abbreviation Chart

...	Repeat the stitches within the asterisks as many times as indicated; in the example given, the stitches within the asterisks would be crocheted a total of 3 times.
BBO	Back Bump(s) only, insert hook into the back bumps of a chain
BEG	Beginning
BLO	Back loops only
CH	Chain
DC	Double crochet
DEC	Invisible decrease
DTR	Double Triple Crochet or Double Treble Crochet
FC	Foundation chain
FLO	Front loops only
FO	Fasten off
HDC	Half double crochet
IFO	Invisible fasten off
ML	Magic adjustable loop
R1	Row number, for pieces worked in back-and-forth lines
Rnd1	Round number, for pieces worked in continuous spiral rounds
SC	Single crochet
SC2TOG	Single crochet two stitches together (used when Invisible Decrease is not possible)
SL ST	Slip stitch
TC	Triple Crochet

About this Kit

The Crochet Stitches section gives you instructions for every crochet stitch used in this book. The Amigurumi Techniques section includes helpful tips for making three-dimensional shapes. The Embroidery and Sewing Stitches section gives instructions for making face details, Cutie Marks, and knots. The Projects sections includes twelve crochet patterns. These crochet patterns are intermediate-to-advanced level. If you are completely new to crochet, before you begin the patterns in this book, I recommend that you watch internet tutorial videos or sit down with an experienced crocheter to get comfortable with holding the hook with your dominant hand while controlling yarn tension with the other hand, and learning the basic stitches including chain, slip stitch, and single crochet.

What's Included

This kit provides the materials needed to make two amigurumi projects: Twilight Sparkle and Rainbow Dash. The following materials are included: one size C/2.75 mm crochet hook, tapestry needle, embroidery needle, yarn, acrylic felt, embroidery floss, sewing thread, and stuffing.

For tools, you will need scissors, glue, tracing paper, ballpoint pen, and large-headed pins.

To make the remaining 10 projects, you will need to purchase additional yarn, felt, polyester fiberfill stuffing, sewing thread, and embroidery floss. Materials can be purchased at craft supply stores or ordered online from craft retailers' websites.

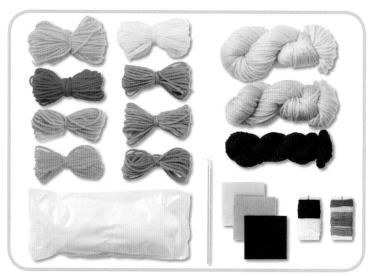

Finished Sizes

About 6.5 inches (17 cm) tall for the ponies, and 4.5 inches (11 cm) tall for Grubber and Spike. Depending on your tension and yarn choice, finished size may vary slightly.

Gauge and Tension

With a C/2.75 mm hook and DK/3/medium weight yarn, my gauge is 10 sc × 10 rows = 1.75 inches (4.5 cm) square. Ideally, when crocheting rounds, you will want snug, dense stitches that will not show the stuffing, but not so tight that you can't get your hook into the next stitch. When you are making pieces in rows, such as the manes and forelocks, your tension can be a bit more loose.

If your stitches are too loose with a C hook, try a 2.5 mm hook. If your tension is very tight—making it difficult to get the hook through the loops—try a D/3.25 mm hook.

If you are a beginning crocheter, I recommend making the pony patterns with worsted weight/4/medium acrylic yarn (such at Red Heart Super Saver acrylic) and an E/3.5mm hook, rather than DK/3/medium weight yarn and D/3.25mm hook. (DK stands for Double Knit.) The bigger size hook and yarn will be easier to work with. With the worsted weight yarn, your finished pony will be one to two inches taller than the pattern's given height. (You will need to enlarge the cutting templates to fit your larger ponies.)

Tools and Materials

Yarn and Thread

When selecting yarn, be sure to choose DK/3/medium weight yarn. Acrylic yarn is my favorite fiber for amigurumi because it's soft, springy, sturdy, economical, and comes in a wide variety of colors. Different yarn brands vary in thickness and sheen, so whenever possible, use the same brand for all the colors of a project. For a list of the brands and colors I used for the projects in this book, see the Recommended Materials section on page 92.

Use six-strand embroidery floss to add details such as nose, mouth, eyelashes, eye highlights, and Cutie Marks. Cut a length of floss and separate strands. Use the number of strands specified in the instructions.

Hooks, Pins, and Needles

All of the patterns in this book are designed to be crocheted with a C/2.75 mm crochet hook. When it's time to sew pieces together, use long pins with large heads to hold everything in place (shorter small-headed pins may disappear between the stitches into the stuffing). Use a tapestry needle, such as the needle in this kit, to sew pieces together, weave in ends, and create face details. A small embroidery needle is useful for stitching the eye highlights onto felt. For stitching the tiny Cutie Marks, a "quilting applique sharp" needle with an eye just big enough to fit two strands of floss works best.

Stitch Markers

Use stitch markers to keep track of the first stitch in a row or round. You can purchase stitch markers at craft stores or improvise with a safety pin or a scrap of yarn in a contrasting color.

Miscellaneous Materials

FOR CUTIE MARKS:

- White or light-colored tissue paper for tracing templates
- Ballpoint pen for tracing templates
- Cotton/polyester sewing thread to match pony body
- Small quilting needle
- Small, sharp embroidery scissors
- Small scraps of acrylic felt in black, white, light purple, dark purple, turquoise, orange, yellow, pink, and fuchsia to match pony body
- Craft glue for gluing felt eyes to head
- Optional: tweezers
- Optional: fusible interfacing and iron

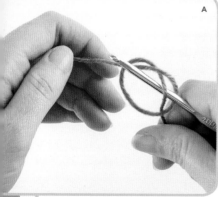

STITCHES & TECHNIQUES

This book uses US crochet terminology, which differs from UK terms; for example, a US single crochet is a double crochet in the UK. So, if you are accustomed to UK terms, here is a conversion chart.

US	UK
chain (ch)	chain (ch)
single crochet (sc)	double crochet (dc)
double crochet (dc)	treble (tr)
half double crochet (hdc)	half treble (htr)
triple crochet (tc)	double treble (dtr)
double triple crochet (dtr)	triple treble (ttr)
slip stitch (sl st)	slip stitch (sl st)

Crochet Stitches

Whether you are a crochet novice or an amigurumi expert, it's a good idea to review and practice the following stitches and techniques before beginning any of the projects in this book.

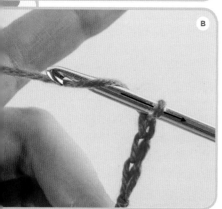

Slipknot

The starting point for most crochet work including the Foundation Chain is a slipknot (however, for starting pieces worked in the round, I recommend the Magic Adjustable Loop or ML, see page 15). To make a slipknot, create a loop by passing the working yarn (the end that leads to the skein) over the tail end (the end that's been cut). Then pass the working yarn across the underside of the loop. From the top, with your hook, grab the portion of the working yarn that's inside the loop and gently pull it part of the way through the loop, creating a new loop. Pull on the tail end with one hand while holding the new loop with the hook to snug up the knot. With the slipknot on the hook, you are ready to begin the pattern. (**Fig. A**)

Yarn Over (YO)

You will Yarn Over at least once for every crochet stitch. With a slipknot on your hook, hold the hook in your dominant hand between your thumb and forefinger with the mouth of the hook facing you and pointed toward your nondominant hand. Use the middle and ring fingers of your nondominant hand to grasp the tail end of the yarn just below the base of the slipknot. Then use the thumb and forefinger of your nondominant hand to pass the working end of the yarn over the top of the crochet hook from back to front.

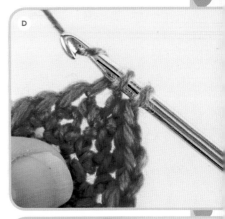

Chain (CH)

To make a chain, begin with a slipknot. YO and then, holding the working end of the yarn taut with your nondominant hand, twist the hook toward yourself slightly so that the YO is captured inside the mouth of the hook. Now pull the tip of the hook with the YO through the working loop and twist it slightly away from yourself. The YO has now become the working loop on the hook. Repeat this process to chain as many stitches as you need. Remember, the working loop (i.e., the loop remaining on your hook after the last stitch in a row or round) does not count toward your stitch total. (**Fig. B**)

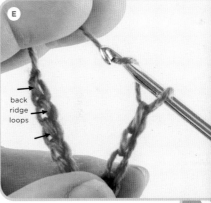

back ridge loops

Foundation Chain (FC)

When you are making a Foundation Chain (FC) such as "FC: Ch 10", make a slipknot, then make 10 chain stitches; however, when you check your stitch count, count the slip knot as the first stitch, while the last loop on the hook (or working loop) does not count as a stitch.

Working Into the Chain

Once you have chained the required number of stitches, pause for a minute to look at the composition of the chain. You'll notice that the front of the chain looks like a series of "V"s, while the back has a ridge of bumps going down the center like a dashed line. Most patterns will specify

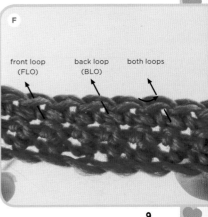

front loop (FLO)   back loop (BLO)   both loops

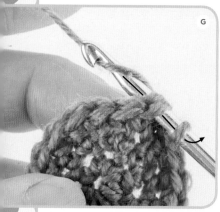

G

skipping the chain closest to the crochet hook and inserting your hook into the second chain from the hook. Insert the crochet hook into the center of the "V" so that the back loop of the V and the back ridge bump are on the hook, with the front loop of the "V" below the hook. Some patterns in this book specify working into the back bumps only (BBO) of a chain; for instructions, see below. (**Fig. C**)

Single Crochet (SC)

The single crochet stitch is the workhorse of amigurumi: you will use this stitch the vast majority of the time for these projects. To begin, insert your crochet hook under the loop or loops of the ch or st. YO and pull the hook through the ch or st. There will now be two loops on the hook. YO again and pull the hook through both loops on the hook to finish the sc stitch. The single crochet stitch is about as tall as it is wide—think of it as a building block or cube. By comparison, slip stitch (below) is half the height of a sc; double crochet is twice as tall as a sc. (**Fig. D**)

H

Working Into the Back Bumps Only (BBO) of a Chain

Some patterns require working into the back bumps of a chain. Insert your hook between the V and the bump on the back ridge of the chain so that the back bump is on the hook and both loops of the V are below the hook. (**Fig. E**)

Working into a Stitch

When you are working into stitches other than chains, such as single crochet, always insert your crochet hook under both loops of the "V"(front and back loops) of the previous round or row, except when indicated in the pattern (BLO or FLO), or if you are using Invisible Decrease (see page 13). (**Fig. F**)

I

Front Loops Only (FLO)

To work into the front loops, insert your hook under the side of the "V" that is closest to you and bring it up in the center of the "V" so only the front loop of the "V" is on your hook. (**Fig. F**)

Back Loops Only (BLO)

To work into the back loops, insert your crochet hook into the center of the "V" and then underneath the side of the "V" that is furthest from you so that only the back loop of the "V" is on your hook. (**Fig. F**)

Slip Stitch (SL ST)

While a single crochet is a two-step process, a slip stitch requires just one step. Insert your crochet hook into a ch or st, YO, and then pull the hook through both the ch or st and the original loop on the hook. This creates a flat stitch with almost no height to it, and it looks like chain lying on top of the previous round or row. Keep in mind a common difficulty with sl sts: we tend to make them tighter than sc; so, when making sl sts, use a little less tension than you normally do. (**Fig. G**)

Half Double Crochet (HDC)

If a slip stitch contributes half as much height as a single crochet, a half double crochet contributes about one and a half times as much height as a single crochet. To make a hdc, YO before inserting the hook into the ch or st. Then insert your crochet hook into the ch or st. YO a second time and pull the hook back through the ch or st. There will now be three loops on the hook. YO a third time and pull the hook through all three loops. (**Fig. H**)

Double Crochet (DC)

A double crochet—twice as tall as a single crochet—is similar to a half double crochet, except that it requires one more YO. First, YO. Then insert your crochet hook into a ch or st. YO a second time and pull the hook back through the ch or st. There will now be three loops on the hook. YO a third time and pull the hook through the first two loops on the hook. There will now be two loops on the hook. YO a fourth time and pull the hook through the last two loops. (**Fig. I**)

Triple Crochet (TC)

A triple crochet stitch is three times as tall as a single crochet. For the first YO, wrap the yarn around the hook twice, so you have two twists and the working loop on the hook shaft. Insert hook into ch or st. YO and pull the hook back through the ch or st. There will now be four loops on the hook. YO and pull the hook through the first two loops on the hook. There will now be three loops on the hook. YO and pull the hook through two loops. Now you have two loops on the hook. YO and pull the hook through the last two loops. (**Fig. J**)

Double Triple Crochet (DTR)

A double triple crochet is the tallest stitch used in this book. It is four times as tall as a single crochet and is used for some of the manes and forelocks. For the first YO, wrap the yarn around the hook three times, so you have three twists and the working loop on the hook shaft. Insert hook into next ch or st. YO and pull the hook back through the ch or st. You will have five loops on the hook. YO and pull the hook through the first two loops on the hook. There will now be four loops on the hook. YO and pull the hook through the next two loops on the hook. There will now be three loops on the hook. YO and pull the hook through the next two loops. Now you have two loops on the hook. YO and pull the hook through the last two loops. (I find it helpful to count "one, two, three" as I wrap the first YO, then I count "one, two, three, four" as I pull the YOs through each pair of loops.) (**Fig. K**)

Increasing

To increase the number of stitches in a row or round and thereby expand the width or circumference of the material, work two or more stitches into one existing stitch or chain. For this book, the majority of increases will be made with single crochet. To increase, make two single crochet stitches within the next stitch, indicated in the patterns as "sc 2 in the next st." (Fig. **L**)

Decreasing

To decrease the number of stitches in a row or round and thereby decrease the width or circumference of the material, work one stitch into two existing stitches or chains. When working in single crochet, this can be done by SC2TOG or Invisible Decrease, as shown below. Whenever you see "dec" in this book, I recommend Invisible Decrease. The SC2TOG method creates a visible difference in a round of sc, but is useful for times when you cannot work the invisible decrease into the front loops of the stitches.

Single Crochet Two Together (SC2TOG)

Insert your hook under both loops of a stitch, YO, and pull the hook through the st. There will now be two loops on the hook. Insert your hook under both loops of the next st. YO a second time and pull the hook through the st. There will now be three loops on the hook. YO a third time and pull through all three loops. (Fig. **M**)

Invisible Decrease (DEC)

The Invisible Decrease, which creates a more uniform sc look than SC2TOG, is best for amigurumi parts worked in the round. Insert your hook into the front loop only of a stitch and then insert your hook into the front loop only of the next stitch. YO and pull the hook through the first two loops on the hook. There will now be two loops on the hook. YO a second time and pull through the remaining two loops. (Fig. **N**)

Fasten Off (FO)

When you complete a piece of a crochet project and have the working loop remaining on your hook, cut the working yarn, leaving several inches for a tail (or more, if indicated, for sewing parts together). Thread the tail through the loop on the hook and pull, cinching the final loop tight around the tail. If the pattern says to weave in the end, using a tapestry needle and the tail, work the needle in the backside of the crochet fabric beneath several stitches (at least 1.5 inches or 4 cm), so the needle does not show in the front. Pull the tail through the stitches, then trim the remaining tail end close to the crochet work, being careful not to cut the crochet work.

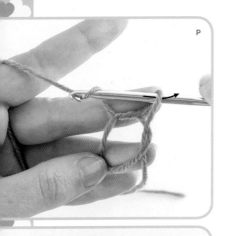

P

RIGHT SIDE   Q

Amigurumi Techniques

If you are familiar with crochet but have not made amigurumi before, this section will acquaint you with helpful techniques specific to forming three-dimensional shapes with yarn.

Working in the Round vs. Working in Rows

Many pieces in this book are crocheted in the round, usually starting with a circle of 6 single crochet stitches. A typical notation for working in the round in amigurumi patterns begins as "ch 2, sc 6 in the 2nd ch from hook." Alternatively, you can begin a circle for working in the round with the Magic Adjustable Loop (also called Magic Circle) as shown next.

To create crocheted material that is worked in straight, back-and-forth lines rather than in continuous spiral rounds, you'll work in rows. This is indicated in the pattern by the end-of-line instructions, "ch 1, turn." At the end of each row, you flip the material over, chain a certain number of stitches (as directed by the pattern) to account for height, skip those chained stitches, and continue crocheting in the next stitch (**Fig. O**). This creates a crochet fabric with a different surface than spiral rounds: the spiral rounds have a right side and a wrong side, while the flat rows alternate the fronts and backs of the stitches on both sides.

Magic Adjustable Loop (ML)

This method—used to begin crocheting into a circle—is perfect for amigurumi because you can lasso your first round of stitches together in a tight circle and avoid the "donut hole" that usually occurs when crocheting into a slip knot. With the palm of your nondominant hand facing you, wrap the working yarn over the top of your fingers, leaving about six inches of tail dangling below your fingers. Wrap the working yarn up and over again, this time turning your hand palm down and crossing the second wrap over the first wrap. Insert your hook under the first wrap and grab the second, pulling the second wrap in a loop under the first wrap. YO and pull through the loop on your hook (**Fig. P**). Tighten up the stitch on your hook. Remove the wraps from your fingers and hold the wraps and tail under the hook in your nondominant hand. Now create the desired number of stitches (usually 6 sc) by working into the wraps that were around your fingers. When finished, pull on the tail end of the yarn to cinch the wraps tightly and bring the stitches together into a circle. Insert your stitch marker and proceed to the second round.

Right Side and Wrong Side

When working in the round, it is important to know which side of the material is the right side and which is the wrong side. As your work begins to form into a cup shape, you'll notice that you're inserting your hook on the inside of the cup. The interior of the cup is the right side. You can tell by looking at the stitches—they appear to be little "V"s. The exterior of the cup is the wrong side; the stitches look like the Greek letter Pi (π), or two legs with a bar across the top. To make sure that the right side faces outward, invert your cup after a few rounds and continue to work, inserting your hook into the outside of the cup. This inversion is especially important before beginning any invisible decreases, as the designation of back loops and front loops will depend on the orientation of your work. (**Figs. Q** and **R**)

Continuous Spiral Rounds vs. Joined Rounds

When working in the round, as is often the case with amigurumi, there are two methods for continuing to the next round: spiral rounds and joined rounds. Working in joined rounds means that at the end of every complete circle of stitches, the first stitch is joined to the last stitch using a slip stitch, then a specified number of chains are made to account for the height of the next round. This creates a visible seam at the points where the rows are joined. Working in continuous spiral rounds is a way to avoid creating that visible seam, but it can be more difficult to keep track of the work because there is no visible beginning or end in each round. To work in continuous

R   WRONG SIDE

S

spiral rounds, no slip stitches or chains are used—simply continue crocheting directly in the next stitch. Keep track of your rounds with a stitch marker or a small piece of yarn in a contrasting color. When you complete a round, count the stitches to make sure it matches the pattern stitch count (given in parentheses at the end of a line), then move the round marker up to the loop/stitch on your hook.

For this book, always use continuous spiral rounds rather than joined rounds unless otherwise indicated. (**Figs. S** and **T**)

Changing Yarn Colors

To change colors, complete the final stitch in the first color up to the point where there are two loops remaining on the crochet hook. Then drop the first color and pick up the new color, using the new color for the final YO. Pull through the last two loops on the hook and continue working with the new color. If you will be changing back to the first color after a few stitches, carry it behind your work. Otherwise, tie off both of the tails behind the work with a square knot (but do not tighten the knot too much to avoid distorting the crochet stitches before and after). When crocheting in spiral rounds, a color switch will create a visible jog or step in the rounds. To hide these color jogs, position the color transitions on the back of the crochet piece when sewing parts together. (**Fig. U**)

Invisible Fasten Off (IFO)

To finish a piece of crochet material (e.g., the pony wings) so that the edge does not have an obvious height transition or knot, work the last sc of the pattern as indicated, then make a slip stitch into the next stitch. Remove the hook and cut the working yarn,

leaving several inches of tail. Instead of inserting the tail into the final loop, pull the loop up until the tail comes through the slip stitch. Thread the tail onto a tapestry needle. Skip the next sc. Insert the needle under both loops of the next stitch. Pull the yarn all the way through. Then insert the needle under the back loop only of the previous slip stitch (**Fig. V**). Pull the tail just snug enough so the last stitch matches the tension and appearance of the surrounding stitches (**Fig. W**). Weave the remaining tail into the wrong side of the work.

Closing a Hole

When a pattern ends with 6 sts in a round, use the tail yarn to close the hole tightly and make a smooth ending. To close the hole, FO with about 8 inches of tail yarn. With a tapestry needle and tail yarn, whipstitch the tail through front loops only of last six sc. Pull end of yarn snug to cinch hole closed, then make an overhand knot and hide tail inside the crochet work: bring the needle out a couple inches away from the hole, then carefully snip the remaining tail yarn close to the crochet work.

Sewing Crochet Pieces Together

Basically, there are three types of amigurumi piece sewing: sewing an open piece to a closed piece, sewing two closed pieces together, and sewing two open pieces together.

To sew an open piece to a closed piece, first, pin the two pieces together, either with large-head pins or with locking stitch markers (or hold the pieces together with your non-dominant hand). Next, thread the tail yarn from the open piece onto a large-eyed tapestry needle, such as the one included in this kit. To begin the seam, insert the needle

x

both loops of the last round of each piece. Do not pull yarn too tightly, as it may distort the crochet work.

Securing and Hiding End Inside Stuffing

To secure the end of the yarn so your seam does not come undone, use the needle to make an overhand knot around a crochet post close to the seam. After making the knot, insert the needle into the stuffing next to the knot, reemerging from the stuffing about two inches away. Pull the yarn snug, hold in place, then use scissors to carefully snip the yarn close to the exit point (making sure not to snip the crocheted work). The yarn end should disappear into the stuffing when you cut the tension.

Crocheting a Narrow Tube

Some of the projects, particularly the Unicorn horns and Spike's arms, start with the first few rounds made with only four sc around. Crochet work this small requires a little extra finessing.

In a ML, sc 4. Sc in each sc around (4 sts). At this point, the two rounds will curl up into a wrong-side-out ball. Remove your hook from the working loop, and with the tips of your fingers or fingernails of both hands, stretch R2 open and push R1 up to make the work turn right-side out, like popping a contact lens from wrong side to right side up. With your fingers, press R1 and R2 sideways to flatten, then roll between your index finger and thumb to set the stitches and make the beginning of the tube shape. Insert hook in working loop and tighten up the working yarn. As you make the 4 sc of R3, turn your work a quarter turn after each stitch—think of the beginning of the narrow tube like the four sides of a French fry.

between the vertical crochet posts on the the closed piece, then insert the needle from back to front under both "V" loops on the open piece. Insert the needle again into the closed piece in the same post hole as before, emerging from the next post hole. Continue to whipstitch in this manner around the circumference of the open piece, with one whipstitch for every crochet stitch around the last round of the open piece.

To sew a closed piece to a closed piece, use a running stitch (see page 19) that goes between the two pieces: insert the needle under a post of one piece and out next to the next post, then repeat on the other closed piece. Pull the yarn snug. Continue the running stitch around the pieces.

To sew two open pieces together use a whipstitch (see page 19) to sew under

Don't bother using a stitch marker for Rounds 1-3 because the work is so small, the stitch marker will just get in the way—simply count your stitches out loud as you go. After you finish R3, add the stitch marker.

Embroidery and Sewing Stitches

Backstitch

The backstitch looks like a series of tight dashes (----). In backstitching, stitches are sewn backwards to the direction of the sewing. For Cutie Mark embroidery, use backstitching to make fine lines and details, and to outline shapes for satin stitching.

1. With the thread on your needle, knot the end of your thread. At the start of the traced line, pull the thread up from the back to the front of the fabric. Pull the thread through up to the knot at the end.

2. Put the needle down through the fabric a fraction of an inch away forward, then bring it up the same stitch distance forward along the traced line. For best results, make as small a stitch as you can. A craft magnifying glass may be helpful.

3. Take a small backward stitch in the fabric, inserting the needle down into the same hole as the end of the previous stitch.

4. Bring the needle up in front of the second stitch at an equal distance.

5. Continue repeating Steps 3 and 4 along the traced line. Keep the stitches tiny and the same width.

6. To finish, bring needle down through fabric, weave needle through stitching on back of work, then trim ends.

Running Stitch

The running stitch looks like a series of spaced dashes (- - - -). Use it to gather

the row ends together. Insert your needle and yarn through the work from front to back and then from back to front, sewing in a straight line. Stitches should be about the length of a single crochet stitch. (**Fig. X**)

Whipstitch

The whipstitch looks like a series of diagonal slash marks (////). Use a whipstitch to close a small hole at the end of a piece or to sew together the edges of two pieces of crocheted material. To join two pieces with a whipstitch, thread the tail end from one piece of work onto a needle and insert the needle near the edge of piece A. Dip the needle down and under the seam, bringing it up just beyond the edge of piece B. Continue in this fashion all along the seam until the pieces are completely joined. (**Fig. Y**)

Satin Stitch

For the Cutie Marks, use the satin stitch to fill in shapes with smooth, flat, parallel lines.

1. First, backstitch an outline of the shape.

2. With your thread on the needle and a knot in the end of the thread, bring the needle up through the fabric at your starting point: start at the widest part of the shape, just outside the backstitched outline.

3. Insert the needle again across from your original entry point, on the opposite side of the outlined shape, just outside the backstitching.

4. Bring the needle up on the side of the shape where you started as close as possible to the first stitch and go back down on the opposite side, always staying outside the backstitched outline (unless otherwise indicated in the pattern).

5. Repeat Steps 3 and 4 to make additional stitches, always coming up and going back down on the opposite side from where your needle came up or went down. When you have filled in one half of the shape, come back to the middle (widest part) and fill in the other half.

Don't pull the stitches too tight or it will pull the fabric in and cause puckering. I recommend stabilizing the fabric first with fusible interfacing. (**Fig. Z**)

Fly Stitch

Used to sew mouths, fly stitch creates a "V" or "U" shape using embroidery floss. Insert your needle from the back of the material to the front in the spot where you'd like the left corner of the mouth to be. Then insert your needle from front to back in the spot where you'd like the right corner of the mouth to be, but do not pull the thread tight—leave a "U" shaped loop in the front. Insert your needle from back to front again, midway between the first

two points, and about ¼ inch below them. Make sure the loop of thread created in the first step is hanging below the needle as it comes up from the bottom point of the mouth. This will create a "V" shape. Lastly, insert the needle from front to back a fraction of an inch below the bottom point of the mouth and pull snug, but without sinking into the crochet work. To secure thread, pull needle through to back of head, then cut thread close to work. (**Fig. Aa**)

Chain Stitch

Bring up the needle at the starting point. Insert it down at the same place, then bring it out a stitch length ahead. Pass the needle through the loop of the working thread and tighten the stitch. Try to make the loops the same length on each stitch.

Overhand Knot

With one piece of yarn, cross the free end over the standing end, creating a loop. Pass the free end under one side of the loop and up through the center, pulling to tighten.

Square Knot

With two pieces of yarn, cross the right piece over and underneath the left piece. Then cross the left piece over and underneath the right piece. Pull to tighten.

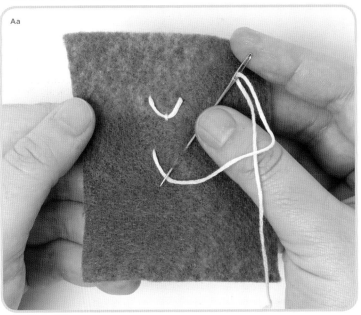

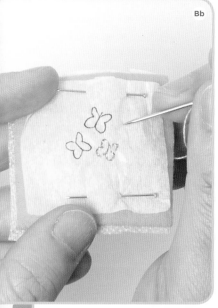

Bb

To Transfer Cutie Mark Design onto Felt:

1. Cut out a 2-inch square of felt. (If you want to embroider on a slighty stiff base, cut out a 2-inch square of fusible interfacing and use warm iron, no steam, to affix to felt.)

2. Using the Cutie Mark templates on page 89, trace the design onto tissue paper or any other easy-to-tear tracing paper with a ballpoint pen.

3. Pin or baste the paper tracing on felt square. (**Fig. Bb**)

To Attach the Cutie Mark:

1. With small, sharp scissors, trim away excess felt around finished embroidered design, leaving about ⅛ inch border around outermost stitching. Trim any long floss ends on back of felt base.

2. Pin embroidered design to finished pony body above rear left leg. With small needle and thread, whipstitch felt base onto body. Hide thread end in body.

MANE 6: BODY TECHNIQUES

Instructions

Foundation Pattern for Pony Head, Ears, Body, and Face

PONY HEAD (WORKED TOP DOWN)

• C/2.75mm hook

Rnd1: Ch 2, sc 6 in 2nd ch from hook or sc 6 in ML. (6 sts)

Rnd2: Sc 2 in each sc around. (12 sts)

Rnd3: *Sc 2 in next sc, sc in next sc*, rep 6 times. (18 sts)

Rnd4: *Sc 2 in next sc, sc in next 2 sc*, rep 6 times. (24 sts)

Rnd5: *Sc 2 in next sc, sc in next 3 sc*, rep 6 times. (30 sts)

Rnd6: *Sc 2 in next sc, sc in next 4 sc*, rep 6 times. (36 sts)

Rnd7: *Sc 2 in next sc, sc in next 5 sc*, rep 6 times. (42 sts)

Rnd8: *Sc 2 in next sc, sc in next 6 sc*, rep 6 times. (48 sts)

Rnd9-20: (12 rounds) Sc in each sc around. (48 sts)

Rnd21: *Sc in next 6 sc, dec*, rep 6 times. (42 sts)

Rnd22: *Sc in next 5 sc, dec*, rep 6 times. (36 sts)

Rnd23: *Sc in next 4 sc, dec*, rep 6 times. (30 sts)

Rnd24: *Sc in next 3 sc, dec*, rep 6 times. (24 sts)

Rnd25: *Sc in next 2 sc, dec*, rep 6 times. (18 sts)

• Stuff Head while slightly pinching middle of Head as you stuff to form a slightly flattened circle. (See **Fig. Cc**)

Cc

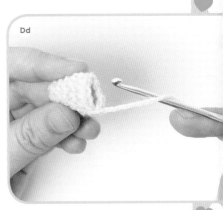

Dd

Rnd26: *Sc in next sc, dec, rep 6 times. (12 sts)

• Sl st in next sc, FO with tail for sewing to Body. Do not close hole.

PONY EARS (WORKED TOP DOWN)

C/2.75mm hook

• Make 2

Rnd1: Ch 2, sc 5 in 2nd ch from hook or sc 5 in ML. (5 sts)

Rnd2: Sc 2 in next sc, sc in next 4 sc. (6 sts)

• Turn crochet work right side out.

Ee

Rnd3: Sc 2 in next sc, sc in next 5 sc. (7 sts)

Rnd4: Sc 2 in next sc, sc in next 6 sc. (8 sts)

Rnd5: Sc 2 in next sc, sc in next 7 sc. (9 sts)

Rnd6: Sc in each sc around. (9 sts)

• Sl st in next sc, FO with tail for sewing to Head. Pinch flat. Leave end open. Do not stuff. (See **Fig. Dd**)

• Pin Ears to Head. With tapestry needle and Ear tail, whipstitch Ear to Head with about 9 or 10 stitches, going around the last round of Ear. Secure end and hide in Head. Repeat for other Ear. (See **Fig. Ee**)

PONY BODY (WORKED FROM BOTTOM TO TOP)
C/2.75mm hook, DK yarn

Rnd1: Ch 2, sc 6 in 2nd ch from hook or sc 6 in ML. (6 sts)

Rnd2: Sc 2 in each sc. (12 sts)

Rnd3: *Sc 2 in next sc, sc in next sc*, rep 6 times. (18 sts)

Rnd4: *Sc 2 in next sc, sc in next 2 sc*, rep 6 times. (24 sts)

Rnd5: *Sc 2 in next sc, sc in next 3 sc*, rep 6 times. (30 sts)

• Rounds 1-5 will form the base of the Pony Body.

Rnd6: In BLO, sc in each sc around. (30 sts)

• Leave an extra stitch marker 3rd sc before end of Rnd6 for leg seam.

Rnd7-13: (7 rounds) In both loops, sc in each sc around. (30 sts)

Rnd14: Dec 4, sc in next 14 sc, dec 4. (22 sts) Leave an extra stitch marker here for Tail placement.

Rnd15: Sc in next 18 sts, dec 2. (20 sts)

Ff

Gg

Rnd16: Dec 2, sc in next 6 sts, dec, sc in next 8 sts. (17 sts)

Rnd17: Sc in next 15 sts, dec. (16 sts)

Rnd18: Dec, sc in next 6 sts, dec, sc in next 6 sts. (14 sts)

Rnd19: Dec, sc in next 10 sts, dec. (12 sts)

Rnd20: Dec, sc in next 10 sts. (11 sts)

• Sl st in next sc, FO with tail. Leave neck open.

ASSEMBLY

1. To make legs, from Rnd6 marker, count 15 stitches around Rnd6 (halfway) and mark remaining front loop of Rnd5 with another stitch marker. Bring the two marked stitches on base together, folding base inward. With tapestry needle and about 15 inches of matching yarn, sew marked stitches together tightly with about 3 or 4 stitches through Rnd6 and Rnd7. This will form a "figure eight" at the base. (See **Fig. Ff**) Remove base stitch markers.

2. Bring yarn up through Rnd6, halfway around the loop from leg seam (about 7 sc from seam). Sew the halfway point of loop into the center of the "figure eight." Next, bring yarn up through Rnd6 on the opposite loop, halfway around (about 7 sc) from the leg seam. Sew the other halfway point of loop into center. This will form a "clover leaf" at the base. (See **Fig. Gg**) Make 2 or 3 stitches through Rnd6 and Rnd7 for the side leg seam. Secure and hide yarn end in body.

3. Pinch off 4 small balls of stuffing. With the eraser end of a pencil, stuff a small ball into each leg. With more stuffing, continue stuffing the Body, using the pencil to insert stuffing. Stuff to medium firmness.

4. If you wish to add structure to the Head and Body, add a plastic straw cut to about 4 inches long into the neck and center of the Body, with about 2 inches of straw protruding from the neck. Insert the protruding straw into the Head opening. Safety note: If pony is intended for a child, omit straw.

5. Pin the last round of the Head to the last round of the Body. With tapestry needle and Head tail, whipstitch the Head to the Body with the straw hidden inside for support. Secure and hide yarn end in Head.

PONY EYES AND EYELASHES

1. With pen or pencil, trace oval cutting template on pages 90–91 onto tissue paper or tracing paper.

2. Pin paper tracing onto black felt. Cut 2 black felt ovals.

3. With 3 strands of white embroidery floss and small embroidery needle, satin stitch highlights onto black felt: 4 parallel stitches for top highlight, 3 shorter parallel stitches for lower highlight. Trim floss ends.

4. Glue eyes to Head at Rnd13 or 14, about 6 to 8 sts apart.

5. With long needle and 6 strands of black floss, make two straight stitches on outside edge of each eye for eyelashes.

PONY MOUTH AND NOSE

• With long needle and 6 strands of embroidery floss in color specified in character's pattern, make a fly stitch for mouth and a straight stitch for nose. Fly stitch instructions on page 20.

TWILIGHT SPARKLE

Twilight Sparkle was a young magic student when Princess Celestia first took her under her wing. Twilight's love of books made her a faithful and loyal pupil, but it wasn't until she opened her heart to true friendship that she discovered her own natural spark. Her dedication to friendship and Equestria earned her a set of wings and the title of Princess Twilight Sparkle, and she now lives in the Castle of Friendship in Ponyville. You can make your Twilight Sparkle with or without wings.

Materials

- ★ C/2.75 mm crochet hook
- ★ DK yarn in light purple, navy blue, dark purple, and dark pink
- ★ Black felt
- ★ Embroidery floss in white and dark purple
- ★ Large-headed pins
- ★ Glue
- ★ Tapestry needle
- ★ Scissors
- ★ Stuffing
- ★ Optional: plastic straw for neck support

Finished size: about 6½ inches

26

Instructions

• Make Mane 6 Head, Ears, and Body in light purple as shown on pages 23–25.
• Make eyes, eyelashes, nose, and mouth as shown on page 25. Use dark purple floss for nose and mouth.

TWILIGHT SPARKLE WINGS

• Make 2
• Finished length: 1 inch
• C/2.75 mm hook
• Work all slip stitches in BBO of chains.
• With light purple, ch 4, sl st in 2nd ch from hook, sl st in next 2 ch, ch 5, sl st in 2nd ch from hook, sl st in next 3 ch, ch 4, sl st in 2nd ch from hook, sl st in next 2 ch, sc in same ch, sc 2 in next chain row end, sc in next chain row end, IFO leaving tail for sewing to Body. (See **Fig. A**)
• Pin Wings to Body with right side of Wing facing out. With tapestry needle and light purple yarn, sew rounded base of Wing to Body with 5 or 6 stitches. Secure and hide end in Body. Repeat for other Wing.

TWILIGHT SPARKLE FORELOCK

• Finished width: 4.5 inches
• C/2.75 mm hook
• Work all stitches in BLO.
FC: With navy blue, ch 7.
R1: Sc in 2nd ch from hook, sc in next 5 ch. (6 sts) Ch 1, turn.
R2: Sc 2 in next sc, sc in next 4 sc, sc 2 in next sc. (8 sts) Ch 1, turn.
R3: Sc in each sc across. (8 sts) Ch 1, turn.

Fig. A

R4: Sc in next 7 sc, sc 2 in next sc. (9 sts) Ch 1, turn.
R5: Sc in each sc across. (9 sts) Ch 1, turn.
R6: Sc in next 8 sc, sc 2 in next sc. (10 sts) Ch 1, turn.
R7: Sc in each sc across. (10 sts) Ch 1, turn.
R8: Sc in next 9 sc, sc 2 in next sc. (11 sts) Ch 1, turn.
R9–12: (4 rows) Sc in each sc across. (11 sts) Ch 1, turn.
R13: Sc in each sc across. (11 sts) Switch to purple. Ch 1, turn.
R14: Sc in next 5 sc, ch 7, turn. (12 sts)
R15: Sc in 2nd ch from hook, sc in next 5 ch, sc in next 5 sc. (11 sts) Switch to dark pink. Ch 1, turn.
R16: Sc in each sc across. (11 sts) Ch 1, turn.
R17: Sc in each sc across. (11 sts) Switch to navy blue. Ch 1, turn.
R18–19: (2 rows) Sc in each sc across. (11 sts) Ch 1, turn.
R20: Sc in next 9 sc, sc2tog. (10 sts) Ch 1, turn.

Fig. B

R21: Sc in each sc across. (10 sts) Ch 1, turn.

R22: Sc in next 8 sc, sc2tog. (9 sts) Ch 1, turn.

R23: Sc in each sc across. (9 sts) Ch 1, turn.

R24: Sc in next 7 sc, sc2tog. (8 sts) Ch 1, turn.

R25: Sc in each sc across. (8 sts) Ch 1, turn.

R26: Sc2tog, sc in next 4 sc, sc2tog. (6 sts) Ch 1, turn.

R27: Sc in each sc across. (6 sts)

• FO with tail for sewing. Weave in short ends.

• With needle and tail, make running stitch across end rows along top edge. (See **Fig. B**) Contrasting yarn shown for demonstration only.) Pull running stitch tail to gather ends together slightly to fit from Ear to Ear on Head. Pin Forelock to Head in front of Ears, with the stripes on the left side of Head. (See **Fig. C**) With needle and navy blue yarn, sew gathered end rows to Head. Secure and hide end in Head.

Fig. C

TWILIGHT SPARKLE HORN

• Finished length: 3/4 inch
• C/2.75 mm hook

Rnd1: With light purple, sc 4 in 2nd ch from hook or sc 4 in ML. (4 sts)

Rnd2: Sc in next 3 sc, sc 2 in next sc. (5 sts)

Rnd3: Sc in each sc around. (5 sts)

Rnd4: Sc in next 4 sc, sc 2 in next sc. (6 sts)

• Sl st in next sc, FO with tail for sewing to Head.

• Do not sew Horn to Head until after

Fig. D

making and sewing Forelock to Head. Pin Horn to Head at Forelock gap, centered between eyes at about Round 9-10. With needle and Horn tail, sew Horn to Head with about 5 or 6 stitches. Secure and hide end in Head.

TWILIGHT SPARKLE MANE

• Finished width: 5 inches
• Creates a series of five connected locks of varied lengths with stripes in the middle lock.
• C/2.75 mm hook
• Work all stitches in BLO
FC: With navy blue, ch 22.
R1: Sc in 2nd ch from hook, sc in next 20 ch. (21 sts) Ch 1, turn.
R2–4: (3 rows) Sc in each sc across. (21 sts)
R5: Sc in each sc across. (21 sts) Ch 26, turn.
R6: Sc in 2nd ch from hook, sc in next 25 ch. (26 sts) Ch 1, turn.
R7–9: (3 rows) Sc in each sc across. (26 sts) Ch 1, turn.
R10: Sc in each sc across. (26 sts) Ch 30, turn.
R11: Sc in 2nd ch from hook, sc in next 27 ch. (29 sts) Switch to dark pink. Ch 1, turn.
R12: Sc in each sc across. (29 sts) Ch 1, turn.
R13: Sc in each sc across. (29 sts) Switch to purple. Ch 1, turn.
R14: Sc in each sc across. (29 sts) Ch 1, turn.
R15: Sc in each sc across. (29 sts) Switch to navy blue. Ch 28, turn.
R16: Sc in 2nd ch from hook, sc in next 26 sts. (27 sts) Ch 1, turn.

R17–19: (3 rows) Sc in each sc across. (27 sts) Ch 1, turn.
R20: Sc in each sc across. (27 sts) Ch 22, turn.
R21: Sc in 2nd ch from hook, sc in next 20 ch. (21 sts) Ch 1, turn.
R22–24: (3 rows) Sc in each sc across. (21 sts) Ch 1, turn.
R25: Sc in each sc across. (21 sts)
• FO with long tail for sewing. Weave in short ends.
• With needle and long tail, make running stitch across end rows. Pull running stitch tail to gather ends together slightly to fit from Ear to Ear on back of Head. Pin Mane to Head in back of Ears, making sure pink and purple stripes of Mane and Forelock meet together between the Ears. (See **Fig. D**) With needle and tail, sew gathered end rows to Head. Pin locks into place on back of head, overlapping edges of locks slightly. With needle and tail, tack locks to Head about midway down from top of head. Secure and hide end in Head.

TWILIGHT SPARKLE TAIL

• Finished length: 2 inches
• C/2.75 mm hook
• Work all stitches in BLO
FC: With navy blue, ch 10.
R1: Sc in 2nd ch from hook, sc in next 8 ch. (9 sts) Switch to purple. Ch 1, turn.
R2: Sc in each sc across. (9 sts) Switch to dark pink. Ch 1, turn.
R3: Sc in each sc across. (9 sts) Switch to navy blue. Ch 1, turn.
R4: Sc in each sc across. (9 sts)

Fig. E

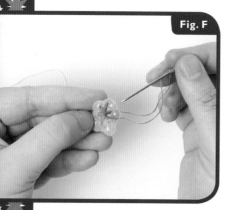

Fig. F

• FO with tail for sewing. Weave in short ends.

• With needle and tail, make running stitch across end rows of one end. Pull running stitch tail to cinch ends together. Secure with 1 or 2 overhand stitches. Sew cinched end to Body at marker. Secure end and hide tail in Body. (See **Fig. E**)

TWILIGHT SPARKLE CUTIE MARK

What You'll Need:

• Light purple felt
• Light purple poly/cotton sewing thread
• Six-strand cotton embroidery floss in white and dark pink
• White or light-colored tissue paper
• Ballpoint pen
• Small, sharp needle (e.g., "quilting applique sharps" with needle eye just big enough to fit 2 strands of floss)
• Tweezers
• Small, sharp embroidery scissors
• Pins
• Optional: fusible interfacing and iron

SEE PAGE 22 TO BEGIN THE CUTIE MARK

1. Cut about 16 inches of dark pink floss. Separate strands. With 1 strand of floss and sharp needle, backstitch along lines through paper and felt, creating outline of big star shape. (See **Fig. F**)

2. With two strands of white floss, stitch through paper and felt to create six smaller stars and accent twinkle lines around big star.

3. After you have finished backstitching the design, carefully tear paper away from stitches. For any tiny, hard-to-remove pieces of paper, gently pull them out with tweezers.

See page 22 to Learn how to FINISH AND attach the Cutie Mark

SPIKE

As Twilight Sparkle's best friend and "number one assistant," Spike relocated from Canterlot to Ponyville to help her learn about friendship. Not only is he loyal and dedicated, he is able to send letters to and from Celestia using his fiery dragon breath! He cherishes his friendships with the ponies—especially his crush, the beautiful Rarity.

Materials

- ★ C/2.75 mm hook
- ★ DK yarn in light purple, light green, and kelly green
- ★ Black felt
- ★ Six-strand cotton embroidery floss in purple and white
- ★ Embroidery needle
- ★ Glue
- ★ Stuffing
- ★ Scissors
- ★ Tapestry needle
- ★ Large-headed pins
- ★ Optional: Plastic straw for neck support

Finished size: about 4½ inches

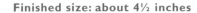

Instructions

HEAD (WORKED TOP DOWN)

Rnd1: With light purple, ch 2, sc 6 in 2nd ch from hook or sc 6 in ML. (6 sts)

Rnd2: Sc 2 in each sc around. (12 sts)

Rnd3: *Sc 2 in next sc, sc in next sc*, rep 6 times. (18 sts)

Rnd4: *Sc 2 in next sc, sc in next 2 sc*, rep 6 times. (24 sts)

Rnd5: *Sc 2 in next sc, sc in next 3 sc*, rep 6 times. (30 sts)

Rnd6: *Sc 2 in next sc, sc in next 4 sc*, rep 6 times. (36 sts)

Rnd7–14: (8 rounds) Sc in each sc around. (36 sts)

Rnd15: *Sc in next 4 sc, dec*, rep 6 times. (30 sts)

Rnd16: *Sc in next 3 sc, dec*, rep 6 times. (24 sts)

Rnd17: *Sc in next 2 sc, dec*, rep 6 times. (18 sts)

Rnd18: *Sc in next sc, dec*, rep 6 times. (12 sts)

• Stuff Head. Pinch head slightly around the middle while stuffing to form flattened oval.

Rnd19: Dec 6. (6 sts)

• FO. Hide end inside Head.

BODY (WORKED BOTTOM UP)

Rnd1: With violet, ch 2, sc 6 in 2nd ch from hook or sc 6 in ML. (6 sts)

Rnd2: Sc 2 in each sc around. (12 sts)

Rnd3: *Sc 2 in next sc, sc in next sc*, rep 6 times. (18 sts)

Rnd4: In BLO, sc in each sc around. (18 sts).

Rnd5–9: (5 rounds) In both loops, sc in each sc around. (18 sts)

Fig. A

Rnd10: *Dec 2, sc in next 5 sc*, rep 2 times. (14 sts)

Rnd11: *Dec 2, sc in next 3 sc*, rep 2 times. (10 sts) Stuff Body.

Rnd12: *Dec 2, sc in next 2 sc*, rep 2 times. (6 sts)

• Sl st in next sc. FO with tail for sewing to Head. Flatten upper body slightly along decreases to form shoulders.

• Pinch base of Body (Rnds1-3) so that Rnd 1 folds to the inside of Body and Rnd3 meets in the middle. With light purple yarn and tapestry needle, sew 2 or 3 stitches to anchor the fold in the middle and create a "figure 8" shaped base. (See **Fig. A**) With needle and yarn, sew back and forth through the pinched middles of Rounds 3 and 4 to create inner leg seam. Secure and hide end in Body.

CHEST SCALES

• With light green, ch 7. In BBO, sl st in 2nd ch from hook, sc in next ch, hdc in next ch, dc in next ch, hdc in next ch, sl st in next ch. FO with tail for sewing to Body.

TAIL

Rnd1: With light purple, ch 2, sc 5 in 2nd ch from hook or sc 5 in ML. (5 sts)
Rnd2: Sc in each sc around. (5 sts) Turn work right-side out.
Rnd3-6: (4 rounds) Sc in each sc around. (5 sts)
• Sl st in next sc, FO with tail for sewing to Body.

TAIL POINT

• With light purple, ch 3. In BBO, sl st in 2nd ch from hook, ch 2, sl st in 2nd ch from hook, sl st in 1st ch. IFO with tail for sewing to Tail Rnd1.

ARMS

• Make 2
FC: With light purple, ch 3.
Rnd1: In BBO, sc in 2nd ch from hook, sc in next sc, turn chain over, in remaining chain loops, sc in next 2 ch. (4 sts)
Rnds2-5: (4 rounds): Sc in each sc around. (4 sts) (Turn crochet work right-side out after Round 2, see page 18 for Crocheting a Narrow Tube.)

• Sl st in next sc, FO with tail for sewing to Body.

LARGE HEAD PLATE

FC: With green, ch 10.
Rnd1: Sc in 2nd ch from hook, sc in next 8 ch, flip ch to opposite side. In top ch loops, sc in next 9 ch. (18 sts).
Rnd2-3: (2 rounds) Sc in each sc around. (18 sts)
Rnd4: Sc in next 7 sc, dec, sc in next 7 sc, dec. (16 sts)
Rnds5-6: (2 rounds) Sc in each sc around. (16 sts)
Rnd7: Hdc in next 3 sc, sc in next sc, sl st in next sc. Do not finish round. FO with tail for sewing to Head. Do not stuff. Pinch flat. If needed, use the end of the crochet hook to push the corners of Rnd 1 out. (See **Fig. B**)

MEDIUM HEAD PLATE

FC: With green, ch 8.
Rnd1: Sc in 2nd ch from hook, sc in next 6 sc, flip ch to opposite side. In top ch loops, sc in next 7 ch. (14 sts)
Rnd2: Sc in each sc around. (14 sts)
Rnd3: Sc in next 3 sc, dec, sc in next 5 sc, dec, sc in next 2 sc. (12 sts)
Rnd4: Sc in each sc around. (12 sts)
Rnd5: Sc in next 5 sc, dec, sc in next 5 sc. (11 sts)
• Sl st in next sc, FO with tail for sewing to Head.

SMALL HEAD PLATE

FC: With green, ch 6.
Rnd1: Sc in 2nd ch from hook, sc in next 4 ch, flip ch to opposite side. In top ch loops, sc in next 5 ch. (10 sts)
Rnd2: Sc in each sc around. (10 sts)

Rnd3: Dec, sc in next 8 sc. (9 sts)

Rnd4: Sc in each sc around. (9 sts)

• Sl st in next st, FO with tail for sewing to Head.

EAR FRILLS

• Make 2

• Work all sl sts in BBO.

• With light green, *ch 4, sl st in 2nd ch from hook, sl st in next 2 ch*, rep 3 times. FO with tail for sewing to Head.

ASSEMBLY

1. For Eyes, cut 2 black felt ovals using cutting template on page 90. With embroidery needle and six strand white floss, satin stitch highlight on black felt eyes: 3 parallel stitches for the top highlight, 2 smaller parallel stitches below for the smaller highlight. Glue eyes onto head about 7 sc apart.

2. Embroider nose and mouth with purple embroidery thread. For nose, make a single straight stitch. For mouth, make a fly stitch. (See page 20 for Fly Stitch.) He looks pretty cute with only the eyes, so feel free to omit the nose and mouth if you prefer.

3. Pin Belly Scales to Body with 1st ch of Scales at top of inner leg seam and other end at last round of Body (neck). With light green yarn and tapestry needle, sew Belly Scales to Body.

4. Pin Large Head Plate to Head with hdcs of Rnd7 facing front and aligning Plate in center of Head between Eyes. Pin Medium Head Plate behind Large Head Plate. Pin Small Head Plate behind Medium Head plate. With tapestry needle and green tail, sew last round of Large Head Plate to Head. Secure and hide end in Head. Repeat for Medium and Small Head Plates. For side view to see scale placement refer to the picture of Spike on page 22.

5. Pin Ear Frills to sides of Head, aligning just above eyes. With tapestry needle and tails, sew base of Frill to Head. Secure and hide ends inside Head.

6. For extra neck support, insert plastic straw (cut to about 3 inches) into stuffing of Head, then insert bottom of straw into neck opening through stuffing of Body. (Do not use straw if figure is intended for small child.)

7. Pin Head to Body with eyes and Belly Scales facing front. With tapestry needle and tail from Body, sew last round of Body to bottom of Head. Secure and hide end inside Head.

8. Pin last round of arm to side of body just below neck. With tapestry needle and tail, sew Arm to Body with about 5 or 6 stitches. Secure and hide end in Body. Repeat for other arm on other side of Body.

9. Pin Tail Point to 1st round of Tail. With tapestry needle and yarn, sew Tail End to Tail with 2 or 3 stitches. Secure and hide end in Tail.

10. Pin last round of Tail to back of Body just above inner leg seam. With tapestry needle and yarn, sew Tail to Body with about 6 or 7 stitches. Secure and hide end in Body.

RAINBOW DASH

No pony in Ponyville can fly as fast as Rainbow Dash! This newly-minted Wonderbolt is very competitive, and she takes every opportunity to show off her soaring skills. As a Pegasus, she is also responsible for the weather and can clear clouds from the sky in ten seconds flat. Her confidence and skill sometimes make her proud and brash, but she has proven herself a true and loyal friend time and time again.

Materials

- ★ C/2.75 mm crochet hook
- ★ DK yarn in turquoise, red, orange, yellow, green, blue, and violet
- ★ Black felt
- ★ Six-strand cotton embroidery floss in blue, white, and black

- ★ Glue
- ★ Tapestry needle
- ★ Scissors
- ★ Large-headed pins
- ★ Stuffing
- ★ Optional: plastic straw for neck support

Finished size: about 6 inches

Instructions

- Make Mane 6 Head, Ears, and Body in turquoise as shown on pages 23–25.
- Make eyes, eyelashes, nose, and mouth as shown on page 25. Use blue floss for nose and mouth.

RAINBOW DASH WINGS

- Make 2
- Finished length: 1 inch
- Work all slip stitches in BBO of chains.
- With turquoise, ch 4, sl st in 2nd ch from hook, sl st in next 2 ch, ch 5, sl st in 2nd ch from hook, sl st in next 3 ch, ch 4, sl st in 2nd ch from hook, sl st in next 2 ch, sc in same ch, sc 2 in next chain row end, sc in next chain row end, IFO leaving tail for sewing to Body. Weave beg tail into wrong side of crochet, trim end.
- Pin Wings to Body with right side of Wing facing out. With tapestry needle and turquoise yarn, sew rounded base of Wing to Body with 5 or 6 stitches. Secure and hide end in Body. (See **Fig. A**) Repeat for other Wing.

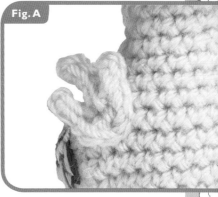

Fig. A

RAINBOW DASH FORELOCK
Lock A

FC: With orange, ch 20.

R1: Sl st in 2nd ch from hook, sc in next ch, hdc in next ch, dc 2 in next ch, tc in next 3 ch, dtr in next 5 ch, tc in next 3 ch, dc 2 in next ch, hdc in next ch, sc in next ch, sl st in end ch, ch 2. (23 sts)

R2: Working in other side of FC loops, sl st in beg ch, sc in next ch, hdc in next ch, dc 2 in next ch, tc in next 3 ch, dtr in next 5 ch, tc in next 3 ch, dc 2 in next ch, hdc in next ch, sc in next ch, sl st in end ch, ch 1. (22 sts)

Fig. B

- FO with tail for sewing. You will have a leaf shape.
- Fold Lock in half lengthwise with wrong side of crochet on outside. With needle and end tail, whipstitch edges together to make a banana shape. (See **Fig. B**) Weave in ends.

Lock B

FC: With red, ch 12.

R1: Sl st in 2nd ch from hook, sc in next ch, hdc in next ch, dc 2 in next ch, tc in next 3 ch, dc 2 in next ch, hdc in next

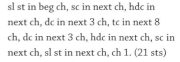

ch, sc in next ch, sl st in end ch, ch 2. (15 sts)

R2: Working in other side of FC loops, sl st in beg ch, sc in next ch, hdc in next ch, dc 2 in next ch, tc in next 3 ch, dc 2 in next ch, hdc in next ch, sc in next ch, sl st in next ch, ch 1. (14 sts)

• FO with tail for sewing.

• Fold Lock in half lengthwise with wrong side of crochet on outside. With needle and end tail, whipstitch edges together. Weave in ends.

Lock C

FC: With yellow, ch 10.

R1: Sl st in 2nd ch from hook, sc in next ch, hdc in next ch, dc in next 3 ch, hdc in next ch, sc in next ch, sl st in next ch, ch 2. (11 sts)

R2: Working in other side of FC loops, sl st in beg ch, sc in next ch, hdc in next ch, dc in next 3 ch, hdc in next ch, sc in next ch, sl st in next ch, ch 1. (10 sts)

• FO with tail for sewing.

• Fold Lock in half lengthwise with wrong side of crochet on outside. With needle and end tail, whipstitch edges together. Weave in ends.

Locks D and E: With orange, make 2 same as Lock C.

RAINBOW DASH MANE
Red Lock

FC: With red, ch 21.

R1: Sl st in 2nd ch from hook, sc in next ch, hdc in next ch, dc in next 3 ch, tc in next 8 ch, dc in next 3 ch, hdc in next ch, sc in next ch, sl st in next ch, ch 2. (22 sts)

R2: Working in other side of FC loops,

sl st in beg ch, sc in next ch, hdc in next ch, dc in next 3 ch, tc in next 8 ch, dc in next 3 ch, hdc in next ch, sc in next ch, sl st in next ch, ch 1. (21 sts)

• FO with tail for sewing.

• Fold Lock in half lengthwise with wrong side of crochet on outside. With needle and end tail, whipstitch edges together. Weave in ends.

Orange Lock

FC: With orange, ch 25.

R1: Sl st in 2nd ch from hook, sc in next ch, hdc in next ch, dc in next 3 ch, tc in next 12 ch, dc in next 3 ch, hdc in next ch, sc in next ch, sl st in next ch, ch 2. (26 sts)

R2: Working in other side of FC loops, sl st in beg ch, sc in next ch, hdc in next ch, dc in next 3 ch, tc in next 12 ch, dc in next 3 ch, hdc in next ch, sc in next ch, sl st in next ch, ch 1. (25 sts)

• FO with tail for sewing.

• Fold Lock in half lengthwise with wrong side of crochet on outside. With needle and end tail, whipstitch edges together. Weave in ends.

Yellow Lock

FC: With yellow, ch 29.

R1: Sl st in 2nd ch from hook, sc in next ch, hdc in next ch, dc in next 3 ch, tc in next 16 ch, dc in next 3 ch, hdc in next ch, sc in next ch, sl st in next ch, ch 2. (30 sts)

R2: Working in other side of FC loops, sl st in beg ch, sc in next ch, hdc in next ch, dc in next 3 ch, tc in next 16 ch, dc in next 3 ch, hdc in next ch, sc in next ch, sl st in next ch, ch 1. (29 sts)

• FO with tail for sewing.
• Fold Lock in half lengthwise with wrong side of crochet on outside. With needle and end tail, whipstitch edges together. Weave in ends.

Green Lock: With green, make same as Yellow Lock.

Blue Lock: With blue, make same as Orange Lock.

Violet Lock: With violet, make same as Red Lock.
• Pin all Locks into place on back of head as shown in **Fig. C**. With needle and turquoise yarn, tack all locks to top of Head between Ears. Tack Mane locks to back of Head about midway down from top of head. Secure and hide end in Head.

Fig. C

RAINBOW DASH TAIL
• C/2.75 mm hook
• Finished length: 1.25 inch
• Make one of each in red, orange, and yellow.

FC: Ch 6.

R1: Sl st in 2nd ch from hook, sc in next ch, hdc in next ch, sc in next ch, sl st in last ch, ch 2. (7 sts)

R2: Working in other side of FC loops, sl st in beg ch, sc in next ch, hdc in next ch, sc in next ch, sl st in last ch, ch 1. (6 sts)
• FO with tail for sewing. Weave in short end.
• Fold piece in half lengthwise with wrong side of crochet on outside. With needle and end tail, whipstitch edges together. Leave long yarn end at point of piece for sewing to Body.

Fig. D

• Pin red, orange, and yellow pieces together as shown in **Fig. D**. With tapestry needle and orange tail, tack three pieces together at end and middles. Hide orange end inside Tail and trim excess.
• Pin Tail to Body above hind legs. With tapestry needle and yellow tail, sew Tail to Body with 2 or 3 stitches. Secure and hide end inside Body. Repeat with red yarn tail.

Fig. E

3. With 2 strands of yellow floss, backstitch through paper and felt to indicate location of yellow bolt.

4. After you have finished backstitching the design, carefully tear paper away from stitches. For any tiny, hard-to-remove pieces of paper, gently pull them out with tweezers.

Satin Stitching and attaching Cutie Mark:

1. With sharp needle and two strands of white, satin stitch cloud *inside* blue floss backstitched outline, starting in middle of cloud with parallel stitches close together, getting narrower as you work down to narrow end. Go back to middle and fill in top half of cloud with parallel satin stitches (See page 20 for Satin Stitch.)

2. With two strands of blue, fill in blue lightning bolt with long parallel stitches. Add detail to center of cloud with three or four short blue backstitches.

3. With two strands of yellow, fill in yellow lightning bolt with long parallel stitches.

4. With two strands of red, fill in red lightning bolt with long parallel stitches.

To finish and attach the Cutie Mark to model, see page 22. See Fig. E for close up of finished Cutie Mark.

RAINBOW DASH CUTIE MARK
What You'll Need:

• Turquoise felt (match Body yarn)
• Turquoise poly/cotton sewing thread (match Body yarn)
• Six-strand cotton embroidery floss in red, yellow, blue, and white
• White or light-colored tissue paper
• Ballpoint pen
• Small, sharp needle (e.g., "quilting applique sharps" with needle eye just big enough to fit 2 strands of floss)
• Tweezers
• Small, sharp embroidery scissors
• Pins
• Optional: fusible interfacing and iron

To begin Cutie Mark, see page 22.

1. Cut about 18 inches of blue floss. Separate strands. With 2 strands of floss and a sharp needle, backstitch along outer cloud shape and blue bolt. (See page 19 for Backstitch.)

2. With 2 strands of red floss, backstitch through paper and felt to indicate location of red bolt.

FLUTTERSHY

Fluttershy, a soft-spoken Pegasus pony, has a special gift of communicating with and comforting all types of animals. Although she and Rainbow Dash grew up together in Cloudsdale, Fluttershy has found she prefers to stay on the ground. Her kindness and gentle ways prove an asset to Ponyville when problems arise.

Materials

- ★ C/2.75 mm crochet hook
- ★ DK yarn in yellow and light pink
- ★ Black felt
- ★ Six-strand cotton embroidery floss in white, black, and dark yellow
- ★ Glue for eyes
- ★ Tapestry needle
- ★ Scissors
- ★ Large-headed pins
- ★ Stuffing
- ★ Optional: DMC Color Infusions Memory Thread in White Luster (a thin copper wire wrapped with thread for shaping Forelock and Mane) and wire cutters
- ★ Optional: plastic straw for neck support

Finished size: about 6½ inches

Instructions

• Make Mane 6 Head, Ears, and Body in yellow as shown on pages 23–25.
• Make eyes, eyelashes, mouth, and nose as shown on page 25. Use dark yellow floss for nose and mouth.

FLUTTERSHY WINGS

• Make 2
• Finished length: 1 inch
• C/2.75mm hook
• Work all slip stitches in BBO of chains.
• With yellow, ch 4, sl st in 2nd ch from hook, sl st in next 2 ch, ch 5, sl st in 2nd ch from hook, sl st in next 3 ch, ch 4, sl st in 2nd ch from hook, sl st in next 2 ch, sc in same ch, sc 2 in next chain row end, sc in next chain row end. IFO, leaving tail for sewing to Body.
• Pin Wings to Body with right side of Wing facing out. With tapestry needle and yellow yarn, sew rounded base of Wing to Body with 5 or 6 stitches. Secure and hide end in Body. Repeat for other Wing.

FLUTTERSHY MANE

• Finished length: about 6.5 inches
• C/2.75 mm hook

FC: With light pink, ch 31.

R1: Lay Memory Thread wire onto chain with 1/2 inch extending past hook. Fold 1/2 inch end of wire around working yarn close to chain. Carrying along wire inside your stitches across row, sc in 2nd ch from hook, sc in each ch across. (30 sts) Ch 1, turn. With wire cutters, cut wire with 1/2 inch extra. To hide end, fold wire end around working yarn and carry along in first few stitches of next row.

R2: Sc in next 29 sc, sc 2 in last sc. (31 sts) Ch 1, turn.

R3: Sc in each sc across. (31 sts) Ch 1, turn.

R4: Sc in next 30 sc, sc 2 in last sc. (32 sts) Ch 1, turn.

R5: Sc in each sc across. (32 sts) Ch 1, turn.

R6: Sc in next 31 sc, sc 2 in last sc. (33 sts) Ch 1, turn.

R7: Sc in each sc across. (33 sts) Ch 1, turn.

R8: Sc in next 32 sc, sc 2 in last sc. (34 sts) Ch 1, turn.

R9: Sc in each sc across. (34 sts) Ch 1, turn.

R10: Sc in next 33 sc, sc 2 in last sc. (35 sts) Ch 1, turn.

R11: Sc in each sc across. (35 sts) Ch 1, turn.

R12: Sc in next 34 sc, sc 2 in last sc. (36 sts) Ch 1, turn.

R13: Fold another 1/2 inch of Memory Thread wire onto working yarn close to stitching. Carrying along wire, sc in each sc across. (36 sts)

• FO with tail for sewing to Head. To FO wire, cut wire at end of row, leaving about 1/2 inch extra. Fold wire over top of last few stitches. With tapestry needle and tail, whipstitch around wire and last few stitches to hide wire end. (See **Fig. A**) Pin angled end rows (ends with sc increases) of Mane to back of Head with Mane R1 at top center of Head R3, just behind Ears. Pin Mane R13 to center back of Head, about Rnd18. (See **Fig. B**) With tapestry needle and light pink yarn, sew end rows to Head. Roll straight

43

Fig. A

edge of Mane up into a curl and sew curl into place, also tacking Mane to back of Head. Secure end and hide in Head.

FLUTTERSHY FORELOCK

• Finished length: about 8.5 inches
• C/2.75mm hook

FC: With light pink, ch 41.

R1: Lay Memory Thread wire onto chain with 1/2 inch extending past hook. Fold 1/2 inch end of wire around working yarn close to chain. Carrying along wire inside your stitches across row, sc in 2nd ch from hook, sc in each ch across. (40 sts) Ch 1, turn. Cut wire with 1/2 inch extra. To hide end, fold wire end around working yarn and carry along in first few stitches of next row.

Fig. B

R2: Sc in next 39 sc, sc 2 in last sc. (41 sts) Ch 1, turn.

R3: Sc in each sc across. (41 sts) Ch 1, turn.

R4: Sc in next 40 sc, sc 2 in last sc. (42 sts) Ch 1, turn.

R5: Sc in each sc across. (42 sts) Ch 1, turn.

R6: Sc in next 41 sc, sc 2 in last sc. (43 sts) Ch 1, turn.

R7: Sc in each sc across. (43 sts) Ch 1, turn.

R8: Sc in next 42 sc, sc 2 in last sc. (44 sts) Ch 1, turn.

R9: Sc in each sc across. (44 sts) Ch 1, turn.

R10: Sc in next 43 sc, sc 2 in last sc. (45 sts) Ch 1, turn.

Fig. C

R11: Fold 1/2 inch of Memory Thread wire onto working yarn close to stitching. Carrying along wire, sc in each sc across. (45 sts)

• FO with tail for sewing to Head. To FO wire, cut wire at end of row with about 1/2 inch extra. Fold wire over top of last few stitches. With tapestry needle and tail, whipstitch around wire and last few stitches to hide wire end.

• Pin straight end rows of Forelock to Head with last stitch of R11 at center of forehead (at about Head R8) and first stitch of R1 at back of Head (at about Head R4). With tapestry needle and light pink yarn, sew Forelock to Head. Curve Forelock over right Ear and pin at an angle on the back of the Head.

• Tack Forelock onto back of Head with 1 or 2 stitches. Secure and hide end in Head. Shape end of Forelock up into a curl. (See **Fig. C**)

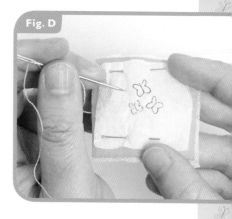

Fig. D

FLUTTERSHY TAIL

• Finished length: 2 inches
• C/2.75 mm hook

FC: With light pink, ch 8.

R1: Sc in 2nd ch from hook, sc in each ch to end of row. (7 sts) Ch 1, turn.

R2: Sk next sc, sc in next 5 sc, sc 2 in last sc. (7 sts) Ch 1, turn.

R3: Sc in each sc across. (7 sts) Ch 1, turn.

R4: Sk next sc, sc in next 5 sc, sc 2 in last sc. (7 sts)

• FO with tail for sewing to Body.

• With needle, weave in beg tail. Pin corner with end tail to Body a few rounds above back leg seam. Sew tail corner to Body with 3 or 4 stitches. Secure and hide end in Body.

FLUTTERSHY CUTIE MARK
What You'll Need:

• Yellow felt (match Body yarn)
• Yellow poly/cotton sewing thread (match Body yarn)
• Six-strand cotton embroidery floss in aqua blue and light pink
• White or light-colored tissue paper
• Ballpoint pen
• Small, sharp needle (e.g., "quilting applique sharps," needle eye just big enough to fit 2 strands of floss)
• Tweezers
• Small, sharp embroidery scissors
• Pins
• Optional: fusible interfacing and iron

To begin the Cutie Mark, see page 22.

1. Cut about 16 inches of light pink floss. Separate strands. With 1 strand of floss and sharp needle, backstitch along lines through paper and felt, creating outlines of butterfly wings (See **Fig. D**) (See page 19 for Backstitch.)

2. With sharp needle and two strands of light pink floss, satin stitch wings with stitches laying in an "x" direction toward center of wings. See Technique section for Satin Stich.

3. With two strands of aqua blue floss, make one long stitch over the center of the butterfly wings, and two small stitches above the wings for antennae.

To finish and attach the Cutie Mark to model, see page 22.

PINKIE PIE

Pinkie Pie has one mission: to bring joy to everypony! When she's not working at Sugarcube Corner bakery making sweet treats or telling jokes, she's planning and throwing parties. You'll know if Pinkie Pie is ever down because her mane becomes flat and lifeless. But as Pinkie Pie knows best, laughter is always the best medicine!

Materials

- ★ C/2.75 mm crochet hook
- ★ DK yarn in light pink and dark pink
- ★ Black felt
- ★ Six-strand cotton embroidery floss in white, black, and dark pink

- ★ Glue
- ★ Tapestry needle
- ★ Scissors
- ★ Large-headed pins
- ★ Stuffing
- ★ Optional: plastic straw for neck support

Finished size: about 6½ inches

Instructions

Fig. A

- Make Mane Six Head, Ears, and Body in light pink as shown on pages 23–25.
- Make eyes, eyelashes, mouth, and nose as shown on page 25. Use dark pink floss for nose and mouth.

PINKIE PIE FORELOCK

- Finished length: 5.5 inches
- C/2.75 mm hook

FC: With dark pink, ch 45.

R1: Sl st in 2nd ch from hook, sl st in next ch, sk next 2 ch, sl st in next ch, sc in next ch, sc 3 in next ch, sc in next 2 ch, tc 4 in each ch to end, sl st in last ch with last 4 tc. FO with tail for sewing to Head.

- Pin Forelock to Head as shown in **Fig. A**. With tapestry needle and tail, tack Forelock to Head in several places along the outer edge of the corkscrew. Secure and hide end in Head.

PINKIE PIE MANE LOCK A

- Finished length: about 2.5 inches
- C/2.75 mm hook

FC: With dark pink, ch 20.

R1: Tc 4 in 3rd ch from hook, tc 4 in each ch across, sl st in last ch. FO with tail for sewing to Head.

- Curve Lock A in a half circle and pin both ends of Lock A between Ears on Head. With tapestry needle and tail, tack Lock A to top of Head at both ends of Lock.

PINKIE PIE MANE LOCK B

- Finished length: about 4 inches
- C/2.75 mm hook

FC: With dark pink, ch 32.

R1: Tc 4 in 3rd ch from hook, tc 4 in each ch across, sl st in last ch.

- FO with tail for sewing to Head.
- Curve in Lock B in half circle and pin both ends behind Lock A on back of Head. With tapestry needle and tail, tack Lock B to Head at both ends of Lock. Tack sides of Lock B to sides of Lock A. Secure and hide end in Body.

PINKIE PIE MANE LOCK C: MAKE SAME AS LOCK A.

- Curve Lock C in half circle and pin both ends behind Lock B. With tapestry needle and tail, tack both ends of Lock C to Head. Tack sides of Lock C to Lock B in several places where they touch. Secure and hide end inside Head.

PINKIE PIE MANE LOCK D: MAKE SAME AS FORELOCK.

- Curve Lock D in a circle with beginning extending past end about 2 inches. Pin flat to lower back of Head under Lock C. (See **Fig. B**) With tapestry needle and tail, tack Lock D to Head in several places. Secure and hide end inside Head.

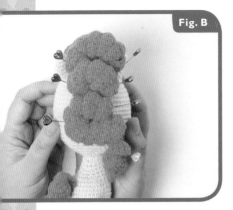

Fig. B

PINKIE PIE TAIL

• Finished Length: 1.5 inches
• C/2.75 mm hook

FC: With dark pink, ch 20.

R1: Sl st in 2nd ch from hook, sl st in next ch, sk next 2 ch, sl st in next ch, sc in next ch, sc 3 in next ch, sc in next 2 ch, tc 4 in next 6 chs, dc in next ch, hdc in next ch, sc in next ch, sc 2 in last ch. FO with tail for sewing to Body.

• Pin end of Tail to Body a few rounds above back leg seam. With tapestry needle and end tail, sew Tail to Body with 3 or 4 stitches. Secure and hide end in Body.

PINKIE PIE CUTIE MARK

What You'll Need:

• Light pink felt (match Body yarn)
• Light pink poly/cotton sewing thread (match Body yarn)
• Six-strand cotton embroidery floss in yellow and aqua blue
• White or light-colored tissue paper
• Ballpoint pen
• Small, sharp needle (e.g., "quilting applique sharps" with needle eye just big enough to fit 2 strands of floss)
• Tweezers
• Small, sharp embroidery scissors
• Pins
• Optional: fusible interfacing and iron

To begin Cutie Mark, see page 22.

1. Cut about 16 inches of yellow floss. Separate strands. With 1 strand of floss and a sharp needle, backstitch around center balloon outline through paper and felt. With 2 strands of yellow, backstitch balloon strings for left and right balloons.

2. Cut about 16 inches of blue floss. Separate strands. With 1 strand of blue floss, backstitch around left and right balloon outline through paper and felt. With 2 strands of blue, backstitch balloon string for center balloon.

3. After you have finished backstitching the design, carefully tear paper away from stitches. For any tiny, hard-to-remove pieces of paper, gently pull them out with tweezers.

SATIN STITCHING:

1. With a sharp needle and 2 strands of yellow floss, starting at the midsection of balloon and working to the top of the outline, fill in balloon outline with horizontal, parallel satin stitches. After filling in top half of balloon, go back to the midsection and fill in bottom of balloon. (See page 20 for Satin Stitch.)

2. With 2 strands of blue, satin stitch over the outlines for the two blue balloon shapes. Stitches for all 3 balloons should lay in the same direction.

See page 22 to finish and attach the Cutie Mark.

APPLEJACK

Applejack is a down-home, farm-raised, salt-of-the-earth pony. She lives on Sweet Apple Acres with her family: Granny Smith; her older brother, Big McIntosh; and her younger sister, Apple Bloom. Applejack's stubbornness and rustic manners are offset by her hard work, dependability, and honesty.

Materials

- ★ C/2.75 mm crochet hook
- ★ DK yarn in yellow, orange, light brown, and red
- ★ Black felt
- ★ Six-strand cotton embroidery floss in white, black, and dark orange

- ★ Glue
- ★ Tapestry needle
- ★ Scissors
- ★ Large-headed pins
- ★ Stuffing
- ★ Optional: plastic straw for neck support

Finished size: about 6½ inches

Instructions

• Make Mane 6 Head, Ears, and Body in orange as shown on pages 23–25.
• Make eyes, eyelashes, nose, and mouth as shown on page 25. Use dark orange floss for nose and mouth.

APPLEJACK FORELOCK

• Finished width: 3 inches
• C/2.75 mm hook
• Make all Forelock stitches in BLO.

FC: With yellow, ch 9.

R1: Sc in 2nd ch from hook, sc in next 7 ch. (8 sts) Ch 1, turn.

R2: Sc in next 7 sc. (7 sts) Ch 3, turn.

R3: Sc in 2nd ch from hook, sc in next ch, sc in next 7 sc. (9 sts) Ch 1, turn.

R4: Sc in next 8 sc. (8 sts) Ch 3, turn.

R5: Sc in 2nd ch from hook, sc in next ch, sc in next 8 sc (10 sts) Ch 1, turn.

R6: Sc in next 9 sc. (9 sts) Ch 9, turn.

R7: Sc in 2nd ch from hook, sc in next 2 ch, sk next ch, sc in next 3 ch, sk next ch, sc in next 9 sc. (15 sts) Ch 1 turn.

R8: Sc in next 8 sc, sk next sc, sc in next 3 sc, sk next sc, sc in next 2 sc. (13 sts) Ch 3, turn.

R9: Sc in 2nd ch from hook, sc in next ch, sc in next 2 sc, sk next sc, sc in next sc, sk next sc, sc in next 8 sc. (13 sts) Ch 1, turn.

R10: Sc in next 13 sc. (13 sts) Ch 2, turn.

R11: Sc in 2nd ch from hook, sc in next 3 sc, sk next 2 sc, sc in next 8 sc. (12 sts) Ch 1 turn.

R12: Sc in next 7 sc, sk next 2 sc, sc in next 3 sc. (10 sts) Ch 3, turn.

R13: Sl st in 3rd ch from hook, sl st in next sc, sc in next 9 sc. (10 sts) Ch 1, turn.

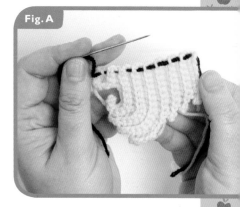

Fig. A

R14: Sc in next 3 sc. (3 sts) Ch 3, turn.

R15: Sc in 2nd ch from hook, sc in next ch, sc in next 3 sc. (5 sts)

• FO with tail.

• With needle and tail, make running stitch through end rows. (See **Fig. A**; contrasting yarn for demonstration only.) Pull yarn to gather ends slightly to about 1.5 inches wide, or to fit space between Ears on Head. Secure end, leave tail for sewing.

• Pin gathered ends of Forelock to Head between Ears. With needle and Forelock tail, sew Forelock to Head between Ears. Secure and hide tail in Head.

APPLEJACK MANE

• Makes a chain of 8 connected locks.
• Finished width: 6 inches
• C/2.75mm hook
• With yellow, *ch 37, tc in 4th ch from hook, tc in next 33 ch*, rep 8 times.
• FO with tail.
• With needle and yellow yarn, make running stitch through attached ends, gather slightly, fold so that wrong side of crochet is on outside and locks are

Fig. B

Fig. C

doubled. Pin attached ends between Ears on back of Head. Sew ends of Mane to Head. Secure and hide end in Head.

• To make tied ponytail, cut 8 inches of red yarn. Lay loose ends of locks together, meeting at the ends and making sure locks are not twisted. Wrap red yarn tightly close to ends of locks (about 1/2 an inch), about 3 or 4 wraps. Secure with a square knot and use needle to hide ends inside ponytail, trimming excess.

APPLEJACK TAIL

• Finished length: 1.5 inches
• C/2.75 mm hook
• With yellow, *ch 10, sc in 2nd ch from hook, sc in next 8 ch*, rep 3 times.
• FO with tail for sewing.
• With wrong side of crochet facing outside, roll together attached end rows. Sew together rolled end and secure, leaving excess tail for sewing to Body.
• Cut 8 inches of red yarn. Lay 3 loose lock ends together. Wrap tightly close to ends with red yarn 3 or 4 times. Secure with a square knot and use needle to hide ends inside Tail, trimming excess.
• Pin rolled end of Tail to Body. With needle and yellow yarn, sew Tail to Body with a few stitches. Secure and hide end in Body. (See **Fig. B**)

APPLEJACK HAT

• Finished diameter: 4 inches
• C/2.75 mm hook
Rnd1: With light brown, ch 2, sc 6 in 2nd ch from hook or sc 6 in ML. (6 sts)
Rnd2: Sc 2 in each sc around. (12 sts)
Rnd3: *Sc 2 in next sc, sc in next sc*, rep 6 times. (18 sts)
Rnd4: *Sc 2 in next sc, sc in next 2 sc*, rep 6 times. (24 sts)
Rnd5: *Sc 2 in next sc, sc in next 3 sc*, rep 6 times. (30 sts)
Rnd6: *Sc 2 in next sc, sc in next 4 sc*, rep 6 times. (36 sts)
Rnd7: In BLO, sc in each sc around. (36 sts).
Rnd8–9: (2 rounds) In both loops, sc in each sc around. (36 sts)
Rnd10: *Sc 2 in next sc, sc in next 11 sc*, rep 3 times. (39 sts)

Rnd11: *Sc 2 in next sc, sc in next 12 sc*, rep 3 times. (42 sts)

Rnd12: In FLO, *sc 2 in next sc, sc in next 6 sc*, rep 6 times. (48 sts) Ch 1, turn.

Rnd13: In both loops, *sc in next 7 sc, sc 2 in next sc*, rep 5 times, sc in next 5 sc. (50 sts, do not finish round. You should have 3 sc remaining to end of round.) Ch 1, turn.

Rnd14: *Sc in next 8 sc, sc 2 in next sc*, rep 5 times, sc in next 4 sc, sc 3 in last sc. (57 sts)

• Continuing in the same direction, crochet into the gap: sc in next end of row, sc in next 3 sc of Rnd12, sc in next end of row, sc 3 in 1st sc of Rnd14.

Rnd15: Continuing in the same direction, *sc in next 9 sc, sc 2 in next sc*, rep 5 times, sl st in next sc. (56 sts) Do not finish round; you should be 2 sc shy of corner.

• IFO, weave in end.

• To make indentation in crown of Hat, pinch underside of Hat at Rounds 3-6 at front center of Hat (lined up with the brim points). Pin about 1/4 inch in from folded edge. With tapestry needle and light brown yarn, sew a few running stitches from center of crown (Round 1) to center front of Round 6. Secure and weave in end. (See **Fig. C**)

• With tapestry needle and light brown yarn, tack Hat onto finished Mane and Head at Hat Round 7. Secure and hide end in Hat.

APPLEJACK CUTIE MARK
What You'll Need:
• Orange felt (match Body yarn)

• Orange poly/cotton sewing thread (match Body yarn)
• Six-strand cotton embroidery floss in red and green
• White or light-colored tissue paper
• Ballpoint pen
• Small, sharp needle (e.g., "quilting applique sharps" with needle eye just big enough to fit 2 strands of floss)
• Tweezers
• Small, sharp embroidery scissors
• Pins
• Optional: fusible interfacing and iron

To begin Cutie Mark, see page 22.

1. Cut about 16 inches of red floss. Separate strands. With 1 strand of floss and a sharp needle, backstitch along lines through paper and felt, creating outlines of apple shapes. (See page 19 for Backstitch.)

2. After you have finished backstitching the design, carefully tear paper away from stitches. For any tiny, hard-to-remove pieces of paper, gently pull them out with tweezers.

SATIN STITCHING AND ATTACHING THE CUTIE MARK:

1. With a sharp needle and two strands of red floss, starting at the middle or apple "core," and working to the rounded edge, fill in the apple outlines with vertical parallel satin stitches, with stitches for all 3 apples laying in the same direction. (See page 20 for Satin Stitch.)

2. With two strands of green, make one small straight stitch for each apple stem and apple leaf. (See **Fig. B** on page 52.)

To finish and attach the Cutie Mark, see page 22.

RARITY

Rarity has an eye for beauty and uses her talent to create fashions at her three boutiques in Equestria. She is a pony of exquisite taste and wants every detail of her designs to be absolutely divine! Believing outer beauty should reflect inner beauty, Rarity is generous with her time and skills to make other ponies sparkle.

Materials

★ C/2.75 mm crochet hook
★ DK yarn in white and dark purple
★ Black felt
★ Six-strand cotton embroidery floss in white and black
★ Glue

★ Tapestry needle
★ Scissors
★ Large-headed pins
★ Stuffing
★ Optional: plastic straw for neck support

Finished size: about 6½ inches

Instructions

• Make Mane 6 Head, Ears, and Body in white as shown on pages 23–25.
• Make eyes, eyelashes, mouth, and nose as shown on page 25. Use black floss for eyelashes, nose and mouth.

RARITY HORN

• Finished length: 3/4 inch
• C/2.75 mm hook
Rnd1: With white, ch 2, sc 4 in 2nd ch from hook or sc 4 in ML. (4 sts)
Rnd2: Sc in next 3 sc, sc 2 in next sc. (5 sts) Turn work right-side out.
Rnd3: Sc in each sc around. (5 sts)
Rnd4: Sc in next 4 sc, sc 2 in next sc. (6 sts)
• Sl st in next sc, FO with tail for sewing to Head. (See **Fig. A**)
• Pin Horn to Head, centered between eyes at about Round 9 or 10. With needle and Horn tail, sew Horn to Head with about 5 or 6 stitches. Secure and hide end in Head.

RARITY FORELOCK

• Finished length: 9 inches
• C/2.75 mm hook
FC: With purple, ch 51.
R1: Sc in 2nd ch from hood, sc in each ch. (50 sts) Ch 1, turn.
R2–9: (8 rows) Sc in each sc. (50 sts) Ch 1, turn.
R10: *Sc in next 2 sc, sc2tog*, rep 4 times, sc to end of row. (46 sts) Ch 1, turn.
R11: Sc in each sc. (46 sts) Ch 1, turn.
R12: Sc in next 6 sc, sc2tog 3 times, sc to end of row. (43 sts) Ch 1, turn.

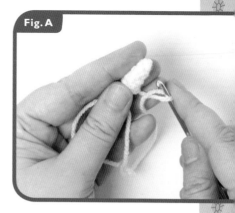

Fig. A

R13: Sc in each sc. (43 sts) Ch 1, turn.
R14: Sc in next 5 sc, sc2tog, sc in next 2 sc, sc2tog, sc to end of row. (41 sts)
• FO, weave in end.
• Pin Forelock to Head with R14 toward back of Head and R1 off center to the left, just behind Horn.
• Curl other end of Forelock up and pin in place. With needle and purple yarn, sew Forelock to Head along Forelock row ends. With needle and purple yarn, tack curl in place with a few stitches along the curled end, then tack Forelock to back of Head with a few stitches. Secure and hide end inside Head.

RARITY MANE

• Finished length: 7 inches
• C/2.75 mm hook
FC: With purple, ch 41.
R1: Sc in 2nd ch from hook, sc to end of row. (40 sts)
R2–4: (3 rows) Sc in each sc across. (40 sts) Ch 1 turn.
R5: Sc in next 28 sc, sc2tog, sc in next 4 sc, sc2tog, sc in next 4 sc. (38 sts) Ch 1, turn.

Fig. B

Fig. C

R6: Sc in next 8 sc, sc2tog, sc in next 28 sc. (37 sts) Ch 1, turn.

R7: Sc in next 28 sc, sc2tog, sc in next 7 sc. (36 sts) Ch 1, turn.

R8: Sc in next 4 sc, sc2tog, sc in next 30 sc. (35 sts) Ch 1, turn.

R9: Sc in next 24 sc, sc2tog, sc in next 9 sc. (34 sts)

• FO with tail for sewing to Head.

• Pin 1st ch of FC behind left Ear, slightly overlapping seam of Forelock, with R9 toward center back of Head. Curl other

end of Mane up and pin to right side of Head. With needle and purple yarn, sew Mane to Head along Mane row ends. With needle and purple yarn, tack curl in place with a few stitches along the curled end, then tack Mane to back of Head with a few stitches. Secure and hide end inside Head. (See **Fig. B**)

RARITY TAIL

• Finished length: 3.5 inches stretched out, 1.5 inches relaxed curl

• C/2.75 mm hook

FC: With purple, ch 20.

R1: Sc in 2nd ch from hook, sc in each ch across. (19 sts)

• FO with tail for sewing to Body. Tail should naturally curl up.

• Pin 1st ch of Tail onto Body a few rounds above the leg seam. With tapestry needle and purple yarn, sew Tail to Body with 3 or 4 stitches. Secure and hide end inside Body. (See **Fig. C**)

RARITY CUTIE MARK

What You'll Need:

• White felt

• White poly/cotton sewing thread

• Six-strand cotton embroidery floss in aqua blue and royal blue

• White or light-colored tissue paper

• Ballpoint pen

• Small, sharp needle (e.g., "quilting applique sharps" with needle eye just big enough to fit 2 strands of floss)

• Tweezers

• Small, sharp embroidery scissors

• Pins

• Optional: fusible interfacing and iron

To begin Cutie Mark, see page 22.

1. Cut about 16 inches of aqua blue floss. Separate strands. With 1 strand of floss and a sharp needle, backstitch along lines through paper and felt, creating outlines of diamond shapes. Make about 3 backstitches for each side of a diamond (See page 19 for Backstitch.)

2. After you have finished backstitching the design, carefully tear paper away from stitches. For any tiny, hard-to-remove pieces of paper, gently pull them out with tweezers.

SATIN STITCHING THE CUTIE MARK:

1. With a sharp needle and two strands of aqua blue floss, satin stitch diamonds, then fill in the diamond outline with parallel satin stitches, with stitches for all 3 diamonds laying in the same direction. (See page 20 for Satin Stitch.)

2. With one strand of royal blue floss, backstitch a smaller diamond outline into the center of each satin stitched diamond. Make a stitch from each corner of aqua diamond to the edge of the centered royal blue diamond (4 sts). Make a stitch halfway between each aqua diamond corner to the edge of the centered royal blue diamond (4 sts).

To finish and attach the Cutie Mark, see page 22.

PRINCESS CELESTIA

Princess Celestia rules over Equestria with her younger sister, Luna. Using her wisdom and powerful magic, she raises the sun each day and maintains peace throughout Equestria. She has taught some of the most gifted Unicorns, including Sunburst, Sunset Shimmer, and (now Princess) Twilight Sparkle.

Materials

- ★ C/2.75 mm crochet hook
- ★ DK yarn in white, pale yellow, rose, teal, light purple, and dark purple
- ★ Black, fuchsia, and yellow felt
- ★ Six-strand cotton embroidery floss in white, black, and taupe
- ★ Glue

- ★ Tapestry needle
- ★ Scissors
- ★ Large-headed pins
- ★ Stuffing
- ★ Tissue paper
- ★ Optional: plastic straw for Head support
- ★ Optional: toothpick or plastic coffee stirrer for Crown support

Finished size: about 7½ inches

58

Instructions

CELESTIA HEAD
(WORKED TOP DOWN)

• Finished height: 4 inches

Rnd1: With white, ch 2, sc 6 in 2nd ch from hook or sc 6 in ML. (6 sts)

Rnd2: Sc 2 in each sc around. (12 sts)

Rnd3: *Sc 2 in next sc, sc in next sc*, rep 6 times. (18 sts)

Rnd4: *Sc 2 in next sc, sc in next 2 sc*, rep 6 times. (24 sts)

Rnd5: *Sc 2 in next sc, sc in next 3 sc*, rep 6 times. (30 sts)

Rnd6: *Sc 2 in next sc, sc in next 4 sc*, rep 6 times. (36 sts)

Rnd7: *Sc 2 in next sc, sc in next 5 sc*, rep 6 times. (42 sts)

Rnd8: *Sc 2 in next sc, sc in next 6 sc*, rep 6 times. (48 sts)

Rnd9: *Sc 2 in next sc, sc in next 7 sc*, rep 6 times. (54 sts)

Rnd10–22: (13 rounds) Sc in each sc around. (54 sts)

Rnd23: *Sc in next 7 sc, dec*, rep 6 times. (48 sts)

Rnd24: *Sc in next 6 sc, dec*, rep 6 times. (42 sts)

Rnd25: *Sc in next 5 sc, dec*, rep 6 times. (36 sts)

Rnd26: *Sc in next 4 sc, dec*, rep 6 times. (30 sts)

Rnd27: *Sc in next 3 sc, dec*, rep 6 times. (24 sts)

Rnd28: *Sc in next 2 sc, dec*, rep 6 times. (18 sts)

• Stuff head while slightly pinching middle of head as you stuff to form slightly flattened circle. (See **Fig. A** in the Techniques section, page 23.)

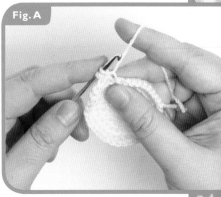

Fig. A

Fig. B

Rnd29: *Sc in next sc, dec, rep 6 times. (12 sts)

• Sl st in next sc, FO with tail for sewing to Body. Do not close hole.

CELESTIA EARS
(WORKED TOP DOWN)

• Finished height: 1.25 inches
• Make 2

Rnd1: With white, ch 2, sc 6 in 2nd ch from hook or sc 6 in ML. (6 sts)

Rnd2: Sc 2 in next sc, sc in next 5 sc. (7 sts)

• Turn crochet work right side out.

Rnd3: Sc 2 in next sc, sc in next 6 sc. (8 sts)

Rnd4: Sc 2 in next sc, sc in next 7 sc. (9 sts)

Rnd5: Sc 2 in next sc, sc in next 8 sc. (10 sts)

Rnd6: Sc in each sc around. (10 sts)

Rnd7: Sc 2 in next sc, sc in next 9 sc. (11 sts)

• Sl st in next sc, FO with tail for sewing to Head. Pinch flat. Leave end open. Do not stuff.

• Pin Ears to Head. With tapestry needle and tail, whipstitch Ear to Head with about 11 or 12 stitches, going around last round of Ear. Secure end and hide in Head. Repeat for other Ear.

CELESTIA LEFT WING

• Finished length: 1.5 inches

• Work all sl sts in BBO.

• With white, ch 3, sl st in 2nd ch from hook, sl st in next ch, ch 4, sl st in 2nd ch from hook, sl st in next 2 ch, ch 5, sl st in 2nd ch from hook, sl st in next 3 ch, ch 6, sl st in 2nd ch from hook, sl st in next 4 ch, ch 1, turn work 1/4 turn clockwise, sc in next 4 remaining ch loops of end rows, FO at beg ch, leaving tail for sewing to Body. Weave in beg tail.

CELESTIA RIGHT WING

• Finished length: 1.5 inches

• Work all sl sts in BBO.

• With white, ch 6, sl st in 2nd ch from hook, sl sl in next 4 ch, ch 5, sl st in 2nd ch from hook, sl st in next 3 ch, ch 4, sl st in 2nd ch from hook, sl st in next 2 ch, ch 3, sl st in 2nd ch from hook, sl st in next ch, ch 1, sc in next 4 end of row ch loops. IFO with tail.

• With needle and tail, weave tail through last 4 sc, emerging at base of shortest chain. Leave tail for sewing to Body. Weave in beg tail.

CELESTIA HORN

• Finished length: 3/4 inch

Rnd1: With white, sc 4 in 2nd ch from hook or sc 4 in ML. (4 sts) (See page 18 for Crocheting a Narrow Tube.)

Rnd2: Sc in next 3 sc, sc 2 in next sc. (5 sts)

Rnd3: Sc in each sc around. (5 sts)

Rnd4: Sc 2 in next sc, sc in next 4 sc. (6 sts)

• Sl st in next sc, FO with tail for sewing to Head.

• Trim excess beg tail. Pin Horn to center of forehead. With needle and tail, sew last round of Horn to head. Secure and hide end inside Head. (Forelock will go on top of Horn, with Horn protruding between gap in stitches.)

CELESTIA BODY
(WORKED FROM BOTTOM TO TOP)

• Finished length: 2.5 inches

Rnd1: With pale yellow, ch 2, sc 6 in 2nd ch from hook or sc 6 in ML. (6 sts)

Rnd2: Sc 2 in each sc. (12 sts)

Rnd3: *Sc 2 in next sc, sc in next sc*, rep 6 times. (18 sts)

Rnd4: *Sc 2 in next sc, sc in next 2 sc*, rep 6 times. (24 sts)

Rnd5: *Sc 2 in next sc, sc in next 3 sc*, rep 6 times. (30 sts)

Rnd6: *Sc 2 in next sc, sc in next 4 sc*, rep 6 times. (36 sts)

• Rounds 1-6 will form base of Body.

Rnd7: In BLO, sc in each sc around. (36 sts) (See **Fig. A**) Switch to white.
• Leave an extra stitch marker at 3rd sc before end of Rnd7 for leg seam.
Rnd8–15: (8 rounds) In both loops, sc in each sc around. (36 sts)
Rnd16: Dec 5, sc in next 16 sc, dec 5. (26 sts)
Rnd17: Sc in next 21 sts, dec 2. (24 sts)
Rnd18: Dec 2, sc in next 6 sts, dec 2, sc in next 10 sts. (20 sts)
Rnd19: Sc in next 18 sts, dec. (19 sts)
Rnd20: Dec, sc in next 15 sts, dec. (17 sts)
Rnd21: Dec, sc in next 6 sts, dec, sc in next 7 sts. (15 sts)
Rnd22: Sc in next 13 sts, dec. (14 sts)
• Sl st in next sc, FO with tail. Leave neck open.
1. To make legs, see page 25, steps 1–3 of assembly.
2. If you wish to add structure to Head and Body, add plastic straw cut to about 4 inches long into neck and center of Body, with about 2 inches of straw protruding from neck. Insert protruding straw into Head opening. Safety note: If pony is intended for child, omit straw.
3. Pin last round of Head to last round of Body. With tapestry needle and Head tail, whipstitch Head to Body with straw hidden inside for support. Secure and hide yarn end in Head.
4. Pin Left and Right Wings to corresponding Body sides above front legs, about midway between base and neck. With tapestry needle and tail, sew short edge of Wing to Body with 3

Fig. C

or 4 stitches. Secure end and hide in Body. Repeat for other Wing.

CELESTIA FACE DETAILS
• Make eyes, eyelashes, nose, and mouth as shown on page 25. Be sure to use the princess eye template on page 90. Use taupe floss for nose and mouth.

CELESTIA FORELOCK
• Finished length: 8 inches
• Work all sts in BLO. Exact stitch count is not important for this piece.
FC: With rose, ch 49.
R1: Sl st in 3rd ch from hook, sl st in next 12 ch, sc in next 10 ch, hdc in next 7 ch, dc in next 6 ch, tc in next 5 ch, dtr to end of row.
• FO rose. Do not turn work.
R2: In BLO, pull up new loop of teal in 3rd sl st from narrow end, sl st in next 6 sts, sc in next 9 sts, hdc in next 6 sts, dc in next 7 sts, tc in next 7 sts, dtr to end of row.
• FO teal. Do not turn work.

R3: In BLO, pull up new loop of light purple in 1st teal sl st, sl st in next 8 sts, sc in next 10 sts, hdc in next 5 sts, dc in next 4 sts, tc in next 5 sts, dtr to end of row.

• FO light purple. Do not turn work.

R4: In BLO, pull up new loop of dark purple in 3rd light purple sl st, sl st in next 3 sts, sc in next 4 sts, hdc in next 5 sts, dc in next 6 sts, tc in next 7 sts, dtr to end of row.

• FO dark purple. Weave in all ends.

• Pin rose row of Forelock to top of Head in front of left Ear, with dark purple row hanging over Horn. Bunch up end rows next to left Ear and pin in place to create pouf. With needle and dark purple yarn, stitch bunched-up end rows of Forelock to Head in front of Ear. With needle and yarn, tack Forelock to Head above right Eye and right cheek to create waves in pointy end of Forelock. Hide end of yarn inside Head.

CELESTIA MANE

• Finished length: 6 inches
• Work all sts in BLO. Exact stitch count is not important for this piece.
FC: With dark purple, ch 35.

R1: Sl st in 2nd ch from hook, sl st in next 5 ch, sc in next 6 ch, hdc in next 6 ch, dc in next 5 ch, tc in next 5 ch, dtr to end of row.

• FO dark purple. Do not turn work.

R2: In BLO, pull up new loop of light purple in 2nd dark purple sl st, sl st in next 6 sts, sc in next 5 sts, hdc in next 6 sts, dc in next 6 sts, tc in next 5 sts, dtc to end of row.

• FO light purple. Do not turn work.

R3: In BLO, pull up new loop of teal in 1st light purple sl st, sl st in next 6 sts, sc in next 5 sts, hdc in next 5 sts, dc in next 5 sts, tc in next 5 sts, dtr to end of row.

• FO teal. Do not turn work.

R4: In BLO, pull up new loop of rose in 2nd dark purple R1 sl st, sl st in next 4 sts, sc in next 6 sts, hdc in next 6 sts, dc in next 6 sts, tc in next 5 sts, dtr to end of row.

• FO rose. Weave in all ends.

• Pin Mane to back of Head with dark purple row on left and rose row on right. Bunch end rows slightly to fit between Ears and pin in place. With needle and rose yarn, sew end rows to Head between Ears, tucking seam slightly underneath rose row of Forelock. Tack middle of Mane to left side of back of Head. (See **Fig. B**) Tack last inch of Mane to left cheek, directly below left Ear. Hide end of yarn inside Head.

CELESTIA TAIL

• Finished length: 1.5 inches
FC: With teal, ch 9.

R1: Sc in 2nd ch from hook, sc in next 7 sc. (8 sts) Switch to rose. Ch 1, turn.

R2: Sc in each sc across. (8 sts)

• FO with tail for sewing.

• Use tails and needle to cinch both end rows to make pointy ends. Secure and weave in short ends, keeping long tail for sewing to Body.

• Pin Tail to Body above rear leg seam. With needle and long end tail, sew Tail to Body with 3 or 4 stitches. Secure and hide end inside Body.

CELESTIA CROWN AND COLLAR

1. Trace crown, collar, and diamond templates from page 91 onto tissue paper.

2. Pin crown and collar tracing to yellow felt. Cut 2 crown shapes and 1 felt collar from yellow felt. Cut 2 diamonds from fuchsia felt.

3. Glue fuchsia diamond to front center of crown. Glue crowns together with toothpick sandwiched between and protruding from bottom edge of crowns.

4. Apply glue to protruding end of toothpick. Insert toothpick into Forelock and Head. (See **Fig. C**) Safety Note: Do not use toothpick if figure is for a small child. Instead, use small needle and yellow thread to whipstitch bottom edge of crown to Forelock and Head.

5. Glue fuchsia diamond to center point of yellow collar. Wrap collar around neck of Body, with point of collar centered above front leg seam. When positioned as you like, glue collar to Body.

CELESTIA CUTIE MARK
What You'll Need:

• Orange felt
• Six-strand cotton embroidery floss in yellow
• White or light-colored tissue paper
• Ballpoint pen
• Small, sharp needle (e.g., "quilting applique sharps" with needle eye just big enough to fit 2 strands of floss)
• Tweezers
• Small, sharp embroidery scissors
• Pins

To begin the Cutie Mark, see page 22.

1. Cut about 18 inches of yellow floss. Separate strands. With 2 strands of floss and sharp needle, backstitch around outline of inner circle. (See page 19 for Backstitch.)

2. After you have finished backstitching design, carefully tear paper away from stitches. For any tiny, hard-to-remove pieces of paper, gently pull them out with tweezers.

Satin stitching the Cutie Mark:

1. With sharp needle and two strands of yellow, satin stitch circle, starting in widest part with horizontal, parallel stitches close together, getting narrower as you work down to edge. Go back to middle and fill in top half with horizontal satin stitch. (See page 20 for Satin Stitch.) Trim any long floss ends on back of felt base.

2. Make second tracing of sun template. Pin on top of satin-stitched design. With small, sharp scissors, trim away excess felt around finished embroidered design, leaving wide circle border around outermost stitching as shown in template.

To finish and attach the Cutie Mark, see page 22.

PRINCESS LUNA

Princess Luna shares responsibility for ruling over Equestria with Princess Celestia, her older sister. It is Princess Luna who raises the moon so that night can come and ponies can rest. Many moons ago, jealousy of her sister caused Luna to turn into a villain called Nightmare Moon. Luckily, Twilight Sparkle and the Elements of Harmony restored Luna and reunited the sisters. Together they maintain harmony in Equestria.

Materials

- ★ C/2.75 mm crochet hook
- ★ DK yarn in dark purple and lavendar
- ★ Black, and white felt
- ★ Six-strand cotton embroidery floss in white, black, and dark blue

- ★ Glue
- ★ Tapestry needle
- ★ Scissors
- ★ Large-headed pins
- ★ Stuffing
- ★ Tissue paper
- ★ Optional: plastic straw for Head support
- ★ Optional: toothpick or plastic coffee stirrer for Crown support

Finished size: about 7½ inches

Instructions

Fig. A

• Use Celestia pattern to make Head, Ears (2), Wings (2), and Horn in the dark purple as shown on pages 59–60. **Fig. A** is a close up of the Princess style wing.

• Sl st in next sc, FO with tail for sewing to Body. Do not close hole.

LUNA BODY
(WORKED FROM BOTTOM TO TOP)

Rnd1: With lavender, ch 2, sc 6 in 2nd ch from hook or sc 6 in ML. (6 sts)

Rnd2: Sc 2 in each sc. (12 sts)

Rnd3: *Sc 2 in next sc, sc in next sc*, rep 6 times. (18 sts)

Rnd4: *Sc 2 in next sc, sc in next 2 sc*, rep 6 times. (24 sts)

Rnd5: *Sc 2 in next sc, sc in next 3 sc*, rep 6 times. (30 sts)

• Rounds 1-5 will form base of Body.

Rnd6: In BLO, sc in each sc around. (30 sts) Switch to dark purple.

• Leave an extra stitch marker 3rd sc before end of Rnd6 for leg seam.

Rnd7-13: (7 rounds) In both loops, sc in each sc around. (30 sts)

Rnd14: Dec 4, sc in next 14 sc, dec 4. (22 sts)

Rnd15: Sc in next 18 sts, dec 2. (20 sts)

Rnd16: Dec 2, sc in next 6 sts, dec, sc in next 8 sts. (17 sts)

Rnd17: Sc in next 15 sts, dec. (16 sts)

Rnd18: Dec, sc in next 6 sts, dec, sc in next 6 sts. (14 sts)

 Rnd19: Dec, sc in next 10 sts, dec. (12 sts)

Rnd20: Dec, sc in next 10 sts. (11 sts)

Fig. B

• Sl st in next sc, FO with tail. Leave neck open. (See **Fig. B**)

• To make legs, see page 25, steps 1–3 of assembly.

• If you wish to add structure to the Head and Body, add plastic straw cut to about 4 inches long into neck and center of Body, with about 2 inches of straw protruding from neck. Insert protruding straw into Head opening. Safety note: If pony is intended for child, omit straw.

• Pin last round of Head to last round of Body. With tapestry needle and

Fig. C

Fig. D

Head tail, whipstitch Head to Body with straw hidden inside for support. Secure and hide yarn end in Head.

• Pin Left and Right Wings to corresponding Body sides above front legs, about midway between base and neck. With tapestry needle and tail, sew short edge of Wing to Body with 3 or 4 stitches. Secure end and hide in Body. Repeat for other Wing.

LUNA FACE DETAILS

1. With ballpoint pen, trace Princess

Eyes cutting template on page 90 onto tissue paper.

2. Pin paper tracing onto black felt. Cut 2 black felt eyes.

3. With 3 strands of white embroidery floss and small embroidery needle, satin stitch highlights onto black felt: 4 or 5 parallel stitches for top highlight, 3 shorter parallel stitches for lower highlight. Trim floss ends.

4. Glue eyes at about Head Rnd13 or 14, about 8 sts apart.

5. With long needle and 6 strands of black floss, make two straight stitches on outside edge of each eye for eyelashes.

6. With long needle and 6 strands of dark blue embroidery floss, make a fly stitch for mouth and a straight stitch for nose. (See page 20 for Fly Stitch.)

LUNA FORELOCK

• Finished length: 8 inches
• Work all sts in BLO. Exact stitch count is not important for this piece.
FC: With lavender, ch 49.
R1: Sl st in 3rd ch from hook, sl st in next 12 ch, sc in next 10 ch, hdc in next 7 ch, dc in next 6 ch, tc in next 5 ch, dtr to end of row.
• FO lavender. Do not turn work.
R2: In BLO, pull up new loop of royal blue in 3rd sl st from narrow end, sl st in next 6 sts, sc in next 9 sts, hdc in next 6 sts, dc in next 7 sts, tc in next 7 sts, dtr to end of row.
• FO royal blue. Do not turn work.
R3: In BLO, pull up new loop of royal blue in 1st royal blue R2 sl st, sl st in next 8 sts, sc in next 10 sts, hdc in next 5 sts, dc in next 4 sts, tc in next

5 sts, dtr to end of row.

• FO royal blue. Do not turn work.

R4: In BLO, pull up new loop of lavender in 1st sl st of R1, sl st in next 3 sts, sc in next 3 sts, hdc in next 5 sts, dc in next 10 sts, tc in next 10 sts, dtr to end of row.

• FO lavender. (See **Fig. C**) Weave in all ends.

• Pin wide end of Forelock R1 to top of Head in front of left Ear, with R4 hanging over Horn. Bunch up end rows next to left Ear and pin in place to create pouf. With needle and lavender yarn, stitch bunched-up end rows of Forelock to Head in front of Ear. With needle and yarn, tack Forelock to Head above right Eye and right cheek to create waves in pointy end of Forelock. Hide end of yarn inside Head.

LUNA SIDELOCK

• Finished length: 3.5 inches

FC: With royal blue, ch 21.

R1: Sl st in 2nd ch from hook, sl st in next 4 ch, sc in next 5 ch, hdc in next 5 ch, dc in next 5 ch.

• FO royal blue. Do not turn work.

R2: In BLO, pull up new loop of royal blue in 2nd sl st of R1, sl st in next 3 sts, sc in next 3 sts, hdc in next 4 sts, dc in next 5 sts, hdc in next 2, sc in next 2 sts.

• FO royal blue. Do not turn work.

R3: In BLO, pull up new loop of lavender in 3rd sl st of royal blue, sl st in next 3 sts, sc in next 3 sts, hdc in next 3 sts, dc in next 8 sts. FO, leaving tail for sewing.

• With wrong side of crochet facing out, pin end of Sidelock to top of Head in front of left Ear. Bunch up

end rows next to left Ear and pin in place. With needle and tail, stitch bunched-up end rows of Sidelock to Head in front of Ear. With needle and tail, tack Sidelock to Head next to left on right cheek. Hide end inside Head.

LUNA MANE

• Finished length: 5.5 inches

FC: With lavender, ch 31.

R1: Sl st in 2nd ch from hook, sl st in next 5 ch, sc in next 3 ch, hdc in next 4 ch, dc in next 7, tc in next 5, dtr to end of chain.

• FO lavender. Do not turn work.

R2: In BLO, pull up new loop of royal blue in 3rd sl of R1, sc in next 4 sts, hdc in next 4, dc in next 5 sts, tc in next 5 sts, dtr to end of row.

• FO royal blue. Do not turn work.

R3: In BLO, pull up new loop of royal blue in 1st st of R2, sc in next 4 sts, hdc in next 6 sts, dc in next 6 sts, tc in next 3 sts, dtr to end of row.

• FO royal blue. Do not turn work.

R4: In BLO, pull up new loop of lavender in 1st sl st of R1, sl st in next 3 sts, sc in next 3 sts, hdc in next 5 sts, dc in next 10 sts, tc in next 10 sts, dtr to end of row.

• FO, leaving tail for sewing.

• With right side of crochet facing out (remaining front loops showing), pin wide end rows of Mane to top back of Head in front of left between Ears. With needle and tail, whipstich wide end rows of Mane to top of Head. Pin narrow end of Mane to the right side of back of Head. Tack Mane to Head at about center of back of Head. Hide end inside Head. (See **Fig. D**)

LUNA TAIL

• Finished length: 1.5 inches
FC: With royal blue, ch 9.
R1: Sc in 2nd ch from hook, sc in next 7 sc. (8 sts) Switch to lavender. Ch 1, turn.
R2: Sc in each sc across. (8 sts)
• FO with tail for sewing.
• Use tails and needle to cinch both end rows to make pointy ends. Secure and weave in short ends, keeping long tail for sewing to Body.
• Pin Tail to Body above rear leg seam. With needle and long end tail, sew Tail to Body with 3 or 4 stitches. Secure and hide end inside Body.

LUNA CROWN AND COLLAR

1. Trace crown, collar, and crescent moon templates from page 90–91 onto tissue paper.
2. Pin crown and collar tracing to black felt. Cut 2 crown shapes and 1 felt collar from black felt. Cut moon from white felt.
3. Glue crowns together with toothpick sandwiched between and protruding from bottom edge of crowns.
4. Apply glue to protruding end of toothpick. Insert toothpick into Forelock and Head. Safety Note: Do not use a toothpick if figure is for a small child. Instead, use a small needle and black thread to whipstitch bottom edge of crown to Forelock and Head.
5. Glue felt moon to center of collar. Wrap collar around neck of Body, with moon of collar centered above front leg seam. When positioned as you like, glue collar to Body.

LUNA CUTIE MARK
What You'll Need:

• Black felt
• Six-strand cotton embroidery floss in white
• White or light-colored tissue paper
• Ballpoint pen
• Small, sharp needle (e.g., "quilting applique sharps" with needle eye just big enough to fit 2 strands of floss)
• Tweezers
• Small, sharp embroidery scissors
• Pins

To begin Cutie Mark, see page 22.

1. Cut about 18 inches of white floss. Separate strands. With 2 strands of floss and sharp needle, backstitch around outline of crescent moon. (See page 19 for Backstitch.)
2. Trim away felt around cloud outline.
3. After you have finished backstitching design and cutting cloud outline, carefully tear paper away from stitches. For any tiny, hard-to-remove pieces of paper, gently pull them out with tweezers.

SATIN STITCHING AND ATTACHING CUTIE MARK:

1. With a sharp needle and two strands of white floss, satin stitch moon, starting in widest part with horizontal, parallel stitches close together, getting narrower as you work down to edge. Go back to middle and fill in top half with parallel satin stitches. (See page 20 for Satin Stitch.) Trim any long floss ends on back of felt base.
2. Glue embroidered design to finished Body above rear leg.

PRINCESS CADANCE

Princess Cadance protects the Crystal Empire with her husband, Shining Armor. She's a kind and wise leader who uses her magic to serve her subjects. Cadance developed her leadership skills while studying with Princess Celestia in her youth, and also shares a special bond with Twilight Sparkle as her former foal-sitter. Now, as mother to Flurry Heart, Cadance dedicates herself to both kingdom and family.

Materials

- ★ C/2.75 mm crochet hook
- ★ DK yarn in pale pink, pale yellow, fuchsia, and violet
- ★ Black, yellow, and fuchsia felt
- ★ Six-strand cotton embroidery floss in white, orange, teal and dark pink
- ★ Glue

- ★ Tapestry needle
- ★ Scissors
- ★ Large-headed pins
- ★ Stuffing
- ★ Optional: plastic straw for Head support
- ★ Optional: toothpick for Crown support

Finished size: about 6½ inches

Instructions

- Use Celesia pattern to make Head, Ears (2), Wings (2), and Horn in white as shown on pages 59–60.
- Use Celestia pattern to make body starting with light yellow for Rn 1-6 then switching to white.
- Make eyes, eyelashes, nose and mouth as shown on page 25. Be sure to use the Princess eye template. Use dark pink floss to make nose and mouth.

CADANCE TOP FORELOCK

- Finished length: 9.5
- Work all sts in BLO. Exact stitch count is not important for this piece.

FC: With pale yellow, ch 50.

R1: Sl st in 2nd ch from hook, sl st in next ch, sc in next 8 ch, hdc in next 4 ch, dc in next 4 ch, tc in next 4 ch, dtr to end of row.

- FO pale yellow. Do not turn work.

R2: Pull up new loop of fuchsia in BLO of 2nd st of R1, sl st in next 2 sts, sc in next 2 sts, hdc in next 2 sts, dc in next 2 sts, tc in next 3 sts, dtr to end of row.

- FO fuchsia. Do not turn work.

R3: Pull up new loop of violet in BLO of 2nd fuchsia st, sl st in next 2 sts, sc in next 2 sts, hdc in next 2 sts, dc in next 2 sts, tc in next 3 sts, dtr to end of row.

- FO violet.
- Weave in all ends. Roll up last 2 inches of narrow yellow end into spiral and pin in place.

CADANCE BOTTOM FORELOCK

- Finished length: 9.5 inches
- Work all sts in BLO. Exact stitch count is not important for this piece.

FC: With violet, ch 50.

R1: Sl st in 2nd ch from hook, sl st in next ch, sc in next 10 ch, hdc in next 4 ch, dc in next 4 ch, tc in next 4 ch, dtr to end of row.

- FO violet. Do not turn work.

R2: Pull up new loop of fuchsia in BLO of 4th st from beg of R1, sl st in next 8 sts, sc in next 5 sts, hdc in next 4 sts, dc in next 4 sts, tc in next 4 sts, dtr to end of row.

- IFO fuchsia.

1. Weave in all ends. With wrong side of crochet facing up, roll up last 2 inches of narrow violet end of Bottom Forelock into spiral and pin in place.

2. With wrong side of crochet facing out, pin wide row ends of Bottom Forelock to top of Head in front of left Ear.

3. With right side of crochet facing out (remaining front loops showing), pin wide row ends of Top Forelock layered on top of Bottom Forelock, overlapping at top of Head and then curving over to left side of Head. Bunch up Top Forelock end rows next to left Ear and pin in place to create pouf.

4. With tapestry needle and violet yarn, sew bunched-up end rows of Top Forelock and Bottom Forelock to Head in front of Ear. With needle and yarn, tack Bottom Forelock to Head above right Eye, then tack Bottom Forelock violet curl to left cheek.

5. With needle and yellow yarn, tack

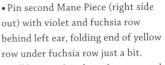

Top Forelock yellow row to Head, sewing down left side of Head, then tack yellow curl to just behind and above violet curl. Hide end of yarn inside Head.

6. With needle and Horn tail, sew last round of Horn to Top Forelock, with 2 or 3 stitches securing Horn to Head through both Forelocks. Secure and hide end inside Head.

CADANCE MANE

• Make 2
• Finished length: 6.5 inches
• Work all sts in BLO. Exact stitch count is not important for this piece.
FC: With violet, ch 38.

R1: Dtr in 6th ch from hook, dtr in next 9 ch, tc in next 4 ch, dc in next 4 ch, hdc in next 4 ch, sc in next 10 ch, sl st in next 2 ch. FO with tail for sewing. Do not turn work.

R2: Pull up new loop of fuchsia in BLO of ch before 1st dtr, ch 6, dtr in next 6 sts, tc in next 3 sts, dc in next 4 sts, hdc in next 4 sts, sc in next 4 sts, sl st in next 8 sts (you will be 3 sts short of end).

• IFO. Do not turn work.

R3: Pull up new loop of pale yellow in BLO of ch before 1st fuchsia dtr, ch 5, dtr in next 7 sts, tc in next 5 sts, dc in next st, hdc in next st, sc in next st, sl st in next st. IFO.

• With right side of crochet facing out (remaining front loops showing), pin wide end rows of one Mane to back of Head with violet row behind right ear and yellow row just left of center of Head.

• Pin second Mane Piece (right side out) with violet and fuchsia row behind left ear, folding end of yellow row under fuchsia row just a bit.

• Roll bottom 2 inches of narrow end of Manes into spiral; pin just above neck at center back of Head and left back of Head.

• With tapestry needle and violet yarn, sew Mane pieces to top of Head along end rows, then tack sides of Manes to back of Head, sewing down to spirals, then tacking spirals to head, laying to left.

• Hide all yarn ends inside Head. (See **Figs. A and B** for reference of how to attach mane and forelocks.)

CADANCE TAIL

• Finished length: 2 inches
Fuchsia and Violet Curl
FC: With fuchsia, ch 19.

R1: Sc in 2nd ch from hook, sc in next 9 ch, hdc in next 2 ch, dc 2 in next sc, dc in next ch, hdc 2 in next ch, sc in next 3 ch. (20 sts) FO.

R2: Pull up new loop of violet in remaining ch loop of 1st ch, sc in next 9 sts. IFO.

• Roll fuchsia sc into spiral and pin together. (See **Fig. C**) With needle and tail yarn, tack spiral together.
Yellow Curl
FC: With pale yellow, ch 15.

R1: Sc in 2nd ch from hook, sc in next 13 sts. (14 sts) FO with tail for sewing.

• Roll sc into spiral and pin together. With needle and tail yarn, tack spiral together. Pin yellow spiral to edge of fuchsia spiral. With needle and tail yarn, sew yellow spiral to fuchsia

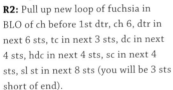

spiral and Tail. Weave in ends.

• Pin Tail to Body above rear leg seam. With needle and fuchsia yarn, sew Tail to Body with 3 or 4 stitches. Secure and hide end inside Body.

CADANCE CROWN AND COLLAR

1. Trace collar, crown front and back, diamond and round jewel templates from page 90 onto tissue paper.

2. Pin crown front and back and collar tracing to yellow felt. Cut crown and collar shapes using traced pattern. Cut diamond and round jewel from fuchsia felt.

3. With small needle and 2 strands of orange floss (about 18 inches), backstitch through tissue and felt along curl outlines on crown front. (See **Fig. D**) (See page 19 for Backstitch.) Carefully remove tissue from Backstitch, using tweezers if needed.

4. Glue fuchsia diamond and round jewel to crown front. Glue crowns together with toothpick sandwiched between and protruding from bottom edge of crowns.

5. Apply glue to protruding end of toothpick. Insert toothpick into Forelock and Head. Safety Note: Do not use toothpick if figure is for small child. Instead, use small needle and yellow thread to whipstitch bottom edge of crown to Forelock and Head.

6. With small needle and 2 strands of orange floss (about 18 inches), backstitch through tissue and felt along curl outlines on collar front. Carefully remove tissue from backstitching, using tweezers if needed. Wrap collar around neck of

Fig. A

Fig. B

Fig. C

73

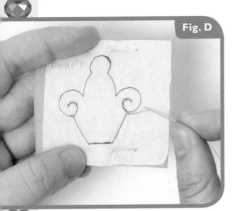

Fig. D

vertical, parallel stitches close together, getting narrower as you work to edge. Go back to middle and fill in other half with vertical satin stitches. (See page 20 for Satin Stitch.) Trim any long floss ends on back of felt base.

To finish and attach Cutie Mark, see page 22.

Body, with point of collar centered at front leg seam. When positioned as you like, glue collar to Body.

CADANCE CUTIE MARK
What You'll Need:
1. Pale pink felt
2. Six-strand cotton embroidery floss in teal and yellow
3. White sewing thread
4. White or light-colored tissue paper
5. Ballpoint pen
6. Small, sharp needle (e.g., "quilting applique sharps" with needle eye just big enough to fit 2 strands of floss)
7. Tweezers
8. Small, sharp embroidery scissors
9. Pins

To begin Cutie Mark, see page 22.

Satin stitching and attaching Cutie Mark:
1. With sharp needle and 2 strands of teal floss, satin stitch heart, entering and exiting needle just outside teal backstitching. Start in center with

TEMPEST SHADOW

This Unicorn with a troubled past seeks to mend her broken horn, but cannot do it alone. While exploring outside Equestria, she forms an alliance with the power-hungry Storm King, who promises to restore her magical horn in return for stealing the magic from the princesses of Equestria. Twilight Sparkle shows Tempest that the greatest magic is found in friendship, and together they defeat the evil Storm King.

Materials

- ★ C/2.75 mm crochet hook
- ★ DK yarn in plum, black, fuchsia, pink, and dark pink
- ★ Black and dark purple felt
- ★ Six-strand cotton embroidery floss in white, teal, and black
- ★ Glue
- ★ Tapestry needle

- ★ Small, sharp needle
- ★ Scissors
- ★ Large-headed pins
- ★ Stuffing
- ★ Optional: plastic straw for neck support
- ★ White or light-colored tissue
- ★ Ballpoint pen
- ★ Optional: tweezers

Finished size: about 7 inches

Instructions

TEMPEST SHADOW BROKEN HORN

• Finished length: 0.5 inch

Pink Core for Horn:

Rnd1: With pink, sc 4 in 2nd ch from hook or sc 4 in ML. (4 sts) (See page 18 for Crocheting a Narrow Tube.)

Rnd2-3: Sc in each sc around. (4 sts)

• FO, close hole, weave in ends.

Outer Horn:

Rnd1: With plum, ch 7, sl st in 1st ch to make loop.

Rnd2: Sc in each ch around. (7 sts)

Rnd3: In BLO, sc2tog, sc in next 4 sc. (6 sts)

Rnd4: In BLO, dc in next sc. Do not finish round. FO, weave in ends.

• Stuff Pink Core inside Outer Horn (See **Fig. A**)

• Pin Horn to Head. With needle and plum yarn, sew FC of Outer Horn to Head.

TEMPEST SHADOW BODY (WORKED BOTTOM TO TOP)

• Finished height: 2.5 inches

Rnd1: With black, ch 2, sc 6 in 2nd ch from hook or sc 6 in ML. (6 sts)

Rnd2: Sc 2 in each sc. (12 sts)

Rnd3: *Sc 2 in next sc, sc in next sc*, rep 6 times. (18 sts)

Rnd4: *Sc 2 in next sc, sc in next 2 sc*, rep 6 times. (24 sts)

Rnd5: *Sc 2 in next sc, sc in next 3 sc*, rep 6 times. (30 sts)

• Rounds 1-5 will form base of Body.

Rnd6: In BLO, sc in each sc around. (30 sts). Switch to plum.

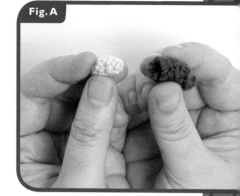

Fig. A

• Leave an extra stitch marker at end of Rnd6 for leg seam.

Rnd7-8: (2 rounds) In both loops, sc in each sc around. (30 sts) Switch to black.

Rnd9-13: (5 rounds) Sc in each sc around. (30 sts)

Rnd14: Dec 4, sc in next 14 sc, dec 4. (22 sts)

Rnd15: Sc in next 18 sts, dec 2. (20 sts)

Rnd16: Dec 2, sc in next 6 sts, dec, sc in next 8 sts. (17 sts)

Rnd17: Sc in next 15 sts, dec. (16 sts)

Rnd18: Dec, sc in next 6 sts, dec, sc in next 6 sts. (14 sts) Switch to plum.

Rnd19: Dec, sc in next 10 sc, dec. (12 sts)

Rnd20: Dec, sc in next 10 sts. (11 sts)

• Sl st in next sc, FO with tail. Leave neck open. (See **Fig. B**)

• To make legs, see page 25, steps 1–3 of assembly.

• If you wish to add structure to Head and Body, add plastic straw cut to about 4 inches long into neck and center of Body, with about 2 inches of straw protruding from neck. Insert protruding straw into Head opening. Safety note: If figure is intended for child, omit straw.

• Pin last round of Head to last round of Body. With tapestry needle and Head tail, whipstitch Head to Body with straw hidden inside for support. Secure and hide yarn end in Head.

TEMPEST SHADOW FACE DETAILS

1. With pen or pencil, trace Princess Eyes cutting template on page 90 onto tissue paper or tracing paper.

2. Pin paper tracing onto black felt. Cut 2 black felt eyes.

3. With 3 strands of white embroidery floss and small embroidery needle, satin stitch highlights onto black felt: 4 or 5 parallel stitches for top highlight, 3 shorter parallel stitches for lower highlight. Trim floss ends. Use same process piece for Celestia Eyes.

4. Glue eyes at about Head Rnd13 or 14, about 8 sts apart.

5. For eyelashes, with long needle and 6 strands of black floss, make three or four stitches close together at outer corner of eye, meeting together at a point to form a triangle. Make a longer stitch angled from beg of bottom stitch up to end of top stitch. Repeat for other eye. Closeup of model eye with eyelashes.

6. For scar, with tapestry needle and dark pink yarn, make one straight stitch above right eye and one straight stitch below right eye. Hide yarn end in Head. (See **Fig. C**)

7. With long needle and 6 strands of black embroidery floss, make fly stitch for mouth and straight stitch for nose. (See page 20 for Fly Stitch.)

TEMPEST SHADOW MANE

• Finished height: 4.5 inches
• Work all stitches in BLO.

FC: With fuchsia, ch 14.

R1: Sc in 2nd ch from hook, sc in next 12 ch. (13 sts) Ch 1, turn.

R2: Sc2tog, sc in next 10 sc, sc 2 in last sc. (13 sts) Ch 2, turn.

R3: Sl st in 2nd ch from hook, sc in next 11 sc, sc2tog. (13 sts) Ch 1, turn.

R4: Sc2tog, sc in next 5 sc. (6 sts) Ch 7, turn.

R5: Sc 2 in 2nd ch from hook, sc in next 5 ch, sc in next 4 sc, sc2tog. (12 sts) Ch 1, turn.

R6: Sc in next 11 sc, sc 2 in last sc. (13 sts) Ch 1, turn.

R7: Sc in next 11 sc, sc2tog. (12 sts) Ch 1, turn.

R8: Sc2tog, sc in next 10 sc. (11 sts) Ch 1, turn.

R9-11: (3 rows) Sc in next 11 sc. (11 sts) Ch 1, turn.

R12: Sc in next 10 sc, sc 2 in next sc. (12 sts) Ch 1, turn.

R13: Sc 2 in next sc, sc in next 10 sc, sc 2 in last sc. (13 sts) Ch 1, turn.

R14: Sc in next 13 sc. (13 sts) Ch 1, turn.

R15: Sc in next 12 sc, sc 2 in last sc. (14 sts) Ch 1, turn.

R16: Sc in next 6 sc. (6 sts) Ch 6, turn.

R17: Sc in 2nd ch from hook, sc in next 4 ch, sc in next 5 sc, sc 2 in last sc. (12 sts) Ch 1, turn.

R18: Sc in next 12 sc. (12 sts) Ch 1, turn.

R19: Sc2tog, sc in next 10 sc. (11 sts) Ch 1, turn.

R20: Sc 2 in next sc, sc in next 8 sc, sc2tog. (11 sts) Ch 1, turn.

R21: Sc in each sc across. (11 sts)

R22: Sc in next 9 sc, sc2tog. (10 sts) Ch 1, turn.

R23: Sc2tog, sc in next 7 sc, sc 2 in last sc. (10 sts) Ch 1, turn.

R24: Sc in next 8 sc, sc2tog. (9 sts) Ch 1, turn.

R25: Sc2tog, sc in next 6 sc, sc 2 in last sc. (9 sts) Ch 1, turn.

R26: Sc in next 7 sc, sc2tog. (8 sts) Ch 1, turn.

R27: Sc2tog, sc in next 5 sc, sc 2 in last sc. (8 sts)

• FO with tail for sewing to Head.

• Pin Mane to Head, with R1 at Horn and last row at center back of Head, close to neck. With tapestry needle and tail, sew Mane to Head. Secure end and hide inside Head.

TEMPEST SHADOW TAIL

• Finished height: 1.5 inches

• Work all stitches in BLO.

FC: With fuchsia, ch 8.

R1: Sc in 2nd ch from hook, sc in next 6 ch. (7 sts) Ch 1, turn.

R2: Sc2tog, sc in next 4, sl st in last sc. (6 sts) Ch 1, turn.

R3: Sl st in next st, sc in next 2 sts. (3 sts) Ch 4, turn.

R4: Sc in 2nd ch from hook, sc in next 2 ch, sc in next 2 sc, sl st in last st. (6 sts) Ch 1, turn.

Fig. B

Fig. C

R5: Sl st in next st, sc in next 4 sts, sc 2 in last st. (7 sts)

• FO. Weave in ends.

• With needle and fuchsia yarn, sew narrow Tail end to Body.

TEMPEST SHADOW ARMOR PLATES AND COLLAR

1. With tissue paper and ballpoint pen, trace cutting templates for Tempest Shadow collar, knee armor, and hind armor on page 91.

2. Pin paper tracing to dark purple

felt. Cut out pattern pieces including 2 knee armor and 1 hind armor.

3. Wrap collar around neck and overlap ends. Glue top end of collar to lapped end.

4. Glue knee armor felt pieces on forelegs on black rounds.

TEMPEST SHADOW ARMOR DETAIL

1. Cut out 2-inch square of dark purple felt.

2. Using Tempest Shadow Hind Mark template on page 91, trace design onto tissue paper or any other easy-to-tear tracing paper with ballpoint pen.

3. Pin or baste paper tracing onto felt square.

4. Cut about 18 inches of teal floss. Separate strands. With 3 strands of floss and sharp needle, backstitch each line of Storm King Shape with long, straight stitches. (See page 19 for Backstitch.)

5. Cut hexagon template shape around stitching.

6. After you have finished backstitching the design, carefully tear paper away from stitches. For any tiny, hard-to-remove pieces of paper, gently pull them out with tweezers.

7. Glue Hind Mark hexagon above hind leg on Body, aligning with other hind armor felt piece.

GRUBBER

Hedgehog henchman Grubber works as a Storm Guard for the Storm King. He wants to be powerful and mean like Commander Tempest, and he tries to be her sidekick. However, she coldly ignores him when he fails to capture Twilight Sparkle and her friends. After the Storm King's defeat, Tempest reconciles with Grubber, assuring him that he may not be an evil sidekick, but he is a loyal friend who can make everyone laugh.

Materials

- ★ C/2.75 mm crochet hook
- ★ DK yarn in dark gray and light gray
- ★ Black felt
- ★ Embroidery floss in teal and white
- ★ Small embroidery needle
- ★ Tissue or tracing paper
- ★ Ballpoint pen
- ★ Glue
- ★ Stuffing
- ★ Scissors
- ★ Tapestry needle
- ★ Large-headed pins
- ★ Optional: Plastic straw for neck support

Finished size: about 4¾ inches

Instructions

Fig. A

HEAD (WORKED TOP DOWN)

• Finished height: 2 inches

Rnd1: With dark gray, ch 2, sc 6 in 2nd ch from hook or sc 6 in ML. (6 sts)

Rnd2: Sc 2 in each sc around. (12 sts)

Rnd3: *Sc 2 in next sc, sc in next sc*, rep 6 times. (18 sts)

Rnd4: *Sc 2 in next sc, sc in next 2 sc*, rep 6 times. (24 sts)

Rnd5: *Sc 2 in next sc, sc in next 3 sc*, rep 6 times. (30 sts)

Rnd6: Sc in each sc around. (30 sts)

Rnd7: *Sc 2 in next sc, sc in next 4 sc*, rep 6 times. (36 sts)

Rnd8–9: (2 rounds) Sc in each sc around. (36 sts)

Rnd10: *Sc in next 4 sc, dec*, rep 6 times. (30 sts)

Rnd11: *Sc in next 3 sc, dec*, rep 6 times. (24 sts)

Rnd12: *Sc in next 2 sc, dec*, rep 6 times. (18 sts)

Rnd13: *Sc in next sc, dec*, rep 6 times. (12 sts)

• Stuff Head. Pinch head slightly around middle while stuffing to form flattened oval.

Rnd14: Dec 6. (6 sts)

• FO. Hide end inside Head.

BODY (WORKED BOTTOM UP)

• Finished height: 1.5 inches

Rnd1: With dark gray, ch 2, sc 6 in 2nd ch from hook or sc 6 in ML. (6 sts)

Rnd2: Sc 2 in each sc around. (12 sts)

Rnd3: *Sc 2 in next sc, sc in next sc*, rep 6 times. (18 sts)

Rnd4: *Sc 2 in next sc, sc in next 2 sc*, rep 6 times. (24 sts)

Rnd5–7: (3 rounds) Sc in each sc around. (24 sts)

Rnd8: *Sc in next 2 sc, dec*, rep 6 times. (18 sts)

Rnd9: Sc in each sc around. (18 sts)

Rnd10: *Sc in next sc, dec*, rep 6 times. (12 sts)

Rnd11: Sc in each sc around. (12 sts)

• Stuff Body.

Rnd12: Dec 6. (6 sts)

• FO. Leave tail for sewing to Head. (See **Fig. A**)

ARMS

• Make 2

• Finished length: 1 inch

FC: With dark gray, ch 3.

Rnd1: Sc in 2nd ch from hook, sc in next sc, turn chain over. In remaining chain loops, sc in next 2 ch. (4 sts)

Rnd2–5: (4 rounds): Sc in each sc around. (4 sts) (See page 18 for Crocheting a Narrow Tube.)

• Sl st in next sc, FO with tail for sewing to Body.

RIGHT EAR

- Finished height: 1.25 inches

Rnd1: With dark gray, ch 2, sc 6 in 2nd ch from hook or sc 6 in ML. (6 sts)

Rnd2: *Sc 2 in next sc, [hdc, dc, hdc] in next sc*, rep 2 times, sc 2 in next sc, [hdc, dc, ch 2, sl st in 2nd ch from hook, hdc] in next sc.

- FO. Leave gap after last stitch.

LEFT EAR

- Finished height: 1.25 inches

Rnd1: With dark gray, ch 2, sc 6 in 2nd ch from hook or sc 6 in ML. (6 sts)

Rnd2: Sc 2 in next sc, [hdc, dc, ch 2, sl st in 2nd ch from hook, hdc] in next sc, *sc 2 in next sc, [hdc, dc, hdc] in next sc*, rep 2 times.

- FO. Leave gap after last stitch.

TAIL

- Finished length: 1 inch

Rnd1: With dark gray, ch 2, sc 4 in 2nd ch from hook or sc 4 in ML. (4 sts)

Rnd2: Sc in each sc around. (4 sts) Turn work right-side out.

Rnd3: Sc 2 in next sc, sc in next 3 sc. (5 sts)

Rnd4: Sc 2 in next sc, sc in next 4 sc. (6 sts)

Rnd5: Sc 2 in next sc, sc in next 5 sc. (7 sts)

Rnd6: Sc 2 in next sc, sc in next 3 sc, sc 2, sc in next 2 sc. (9 sts)

- Sl st in next sc, FO with tail for sewing to Body. Do not stuff.

FEET

- Finished length: 1.5 inches
- Make 2

Rnd1: With dark gray, ch 2, sc 5 in 2nd ch from hook or sc 5 in ML. (5 sts)

Rnd2: Sc 2 in each sc around. (10 sts)

Rnd3–7: (5 rounds) Sc in each sc around. (10 sts)

Rnd8: Dec 5. (5 sts)

- FO with tail for sewing. Do not stuff.
- With needle and tail, close hole. Pinch flat. Pin Feet to base of Body. With tapestry needle and gray yarn, sew Feet to Body. Secure and hide ends in Body.

HEAD SPIKE A

- Finished height: 1.5 inches

FC: With light gray, ch 9.

R1: Tc 2 in 5th ch from hook, dc in next ch, hdc in next ch, sc in next ch, sl st in last ch, ch 2.

R2: Sl st in 2nd ch from hook, sl st in back loop of 1st FC, sc in next ch, hdc in next ch, dc in next ch, tc 3 in last ch.

- FO with tail for sewing.
- Fold lengthwise with wrong side out. With tapestry needle and tail yarn, whipstitch back loops of edges tog. Weave short tail into work and trim excess. Weave long yarn through work and emerge at wide end of Spike.

HEAD SPIKE B

- Finished height: 2 inches

FC: With light gray, ch 12.

R1: Tc 2 in 5th ch from hook, dc 2 in next ch, dc in next 2 ch, hdc in next 2 ch, sc 2 in next ch, sl st in last ch, ch 2.

R2: Sl st in 2nd ch from hook, sl st in back loop of 1st FC, sc 2 in next ch, hdc in next 2 ch, dc in next 2 ch, dc 2 in next ch, tc 3 in last ch.

- FO with tail for sewing.
- Fold lengthwise with wrong side out. With tapestry needle and tail yarn, whipstitch back loops of edges tog. Weave short tail into work and trim excess. Weave long yarn through work and emerge at wide end of Spike.

HEAD SPIKE C

- Finished height: 1.5 inches
FC: With light gray, ch 10.
R1: Tc 2 in 5th ch from hook, dc 2 in next ch, dc in next ch, hdc in next ch, sc 2 in next ch, st st in last ch, ch 2.
R2: Sl st in 2nd ch from hook, sl st in back loop of 1st FC, sc 2 in next ch, hdc in next ch, dc in next ch, dc 2 in next ch, tc 3 in last ch.
- FO with tail for sewing.
- Fold lengthwise with wrong side out. With tapestry needle and tail yarn, whipstitch back loops of edges together. Weave short tail into work and trim excess. Weave long yarn through work and emerge at wide end of Spike.

HEAD SPIKE D

- Make same as Head Spike A.

BACK & TAIL SPIKES

- Finished length: 2.25 inches
FC: Ch 13
R1: Sl st in 2nd ch from hook, *ch 3, sl st in 2nd ch, ch 1, sl st in next 2 ch*, rep 5 times. FO with tail for sewing to Back and Tail. (See **Fig. B**)

ASSEMBLY

1. Pin Right Ear to right side of Head with notched edge of Ear on right side.

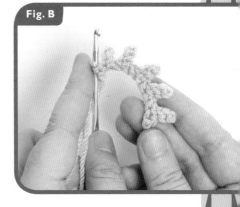

Fig. B

Fig. C

Pin Left Ear to left side of Head with notched edge of Ear on left side. With tapestry needle and yarn, sew Ears to Head. Secure and hide ends inside Head.

2. For Eyes and Nose, cut 1 Nose and 2 Eyes from black felt using cutting template on page 91.
- With embroidery needle and six strand white floss, satin stitch highlight on black felt eyes: 3 parallel stitches for top highlight, 2 smaller parallel stitches below for smaller

highlight. Glue eyes onto head about 4 sc apart. Glue nose between eyes as shown. For eyebrows, with tapestry needle and dark gray yarn, make two long straight stitches just above flat part of felt eye. Repeat for other eye.

3. Chain stitch mouth with 3 strands of black embroidery floss, about 15 to 16 chain stitches. (See page 20 for Chain Stitch.)

4. For teeth, with 3 strands white embroidery floss, make 3 or 4 small, straight, parallel stitches close together just above black chain stitching of mouth for each tooth.

5. Pin Head to Body. With tapestry needle and tail from Body, sew last round of Body to bottom of Head. Secure and hide end inside Head.

6. Pin last round of Arm to side of Body just below seam. With tapestry needle and tail, sew Arm to Body with about 5 or 6 stitches. Secure and hide end in Body. Repeat for other arm on other side of Body.

7. Pin last round of Tail to back of Body. With tapestry needle and yarn, sew Tail to Body with about 9 or 10 stitches. Secure and hide end in Body.

8. Trace shirt template on page 91 onto tissue paper or tracing paper with ballpoint pen. Pin tracing onto black felt. Cut 2 shirt pieces from black felt. Use tracing paper and ballpoint pen to trace Storm King emblem on page 91. Pin emblem tracing to one shirt piece. With embroidery needle and 3 strands of teal floss, stitch through tracing paper and felt to make emblem. Secure floss on back of felt, then carefully tear away tracing paper. Glue Shirt piece with emblem to front of Body. Glue other shirt piece to black of Body.

9. Pin Head Spikes onto Center of Head with Spike seams facing back. Pin Spikes in A, B, C, D order from front to back. With tapestry needle and Spike tail, whipstitch wide end of Spike to Head with 8 or 10 stitches. Secure and hide ends inside Head.

10. Pin Back & Tail Spikes over shirt on back of Body and down to end of Tail. With tapestry needle and yarn, whipstitch flat edge of Spikes to Body and Tail. Secure and hide end inside Body or Tail. (See **Fig. C**)

Cutie Marks

Applejack

Fluttershy

Pinkie Pie

Rainbow Dash

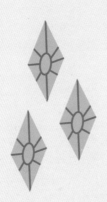

Rarity

Twilight Sparkle

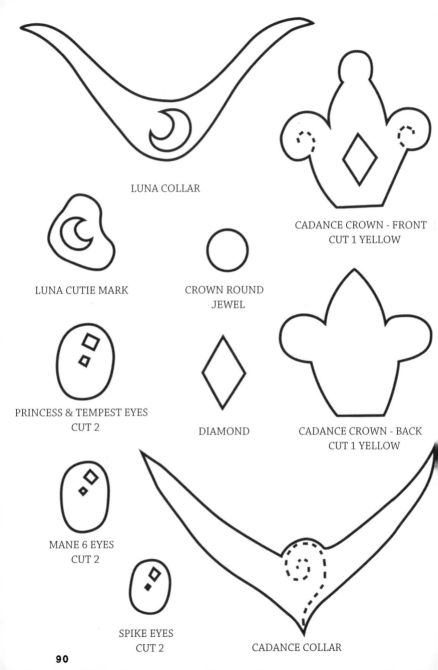

LUNA COLLAR

CADANCE CROWN - FRONT
CUT 1 YELLOW

LUNA CUTIE MARK

CROWN ROUND
JEWEL

PRINCESS & TEMPEST EYES
CUT 2

DIAMOND

CADANCE CROWN - BACK
CUT 1 YELLOW

MANE 6 EYES
CUT 2

SPIKE EYES
CUT 2

CADANCE COLLAR

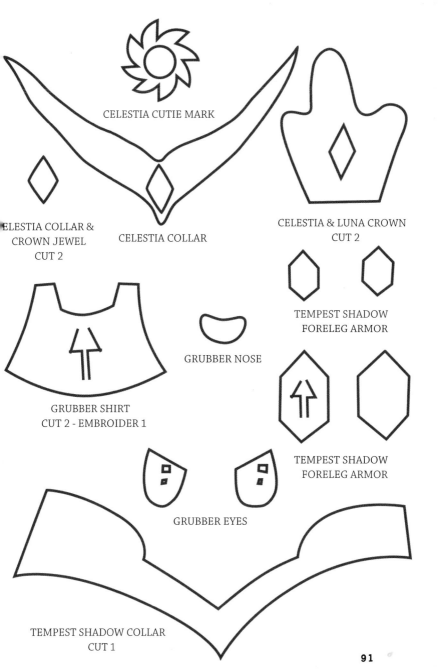

CELESTIA CUTIE MARK

CELESTIA COLLAR & CROWN JEWEL
CUT 2

CELESTIA COLLAR

CELESTIA & LUNA CROWN
CUT 2

TEMPEST SHADOW
FORELEG ARMOR

GRUBBER NOSE

GRUBBER SHIRT
CUT 2 - EMBROIDER 1

TEMPEST SHADOW
FORELEG ARMOR

GRUBBER EYES

TEMPEST SHADOW COLLAR
CUT 1

About the Author

Jana Whitley discovered amigurumi in 2007, and she hasn't put away her hook since. With a background in technical writing and graphic design, Jana found that creating crochet patterns was as much fun as crocheting, and she started writing and selling patterns in her online Etsy store, JanaGeek. Her crochet patterns have been previously published in the *Disney Princess Crochet* and *Soft and Snuggly Cacti*. Jana lives in Utah.

Acknowledgments

A big thank you to Meredith Mennitt and the folks at Quarto for this exciting project. Thanks to Mom for teaching me crochet, embroidery, and countless other arts and crafts. Thanks to Dad for always encouraging an entrepreneurial spirit. Love to the world's sweetest in-laws, Colleen and Tom Whitley. Thanks to my crochet buddy Candace Austin for encouragement. Thanks to my husband for in-home tech support. Finally, I'm grateful to my daughters for introducing me to the delightful, clever world of My Little Pony when they were tiny tots.

Recommended Materials and Tools

If you are searching for an exact match, here are the yarn brands and colors I used:

- Spike the Dragon: Stylecraft Special DK in Wisteria and Spring Green, Lion Brand Bonbons Crayons in Bright Green
- Rarity: Stylecraft Special DK in White and Lobelia
- Fluttershy: Stylecraft Special DK in Citron and Candyfloss, DMC Infusions Memory Thread in White Luster
- Pinkie Pie: Stylecraft Special DK in Candyfloss and Fiesta
- Applejack: Stylecraft Special DK in Citron, Camel, Lipstick, and Saffron
- Rainbow Dash: Stylecraft Special DK in Sherbert, Lion Brand Bonbons Crayons in Bright Orange, True Red, Yellow, Bright Green, Aqua Blue, and Royal Purple
- Celestia: Stylecraft Special DK in White, Lemon, Clematis, Spring Green, Lavender, and Violet
- Cadance: Stylecraft Special DK in Lemon, Soft Peach, Fuchsia Purple, and Violet
- Luna: Stylecraft Special DK in Lobelia, Royal, and Lavender
- Tempest Shadow: Stylecraft Special DK in Plum, Black, Clematis, and Fuchsia Purple
- Grubber: Stylecraft Special DK in Graphite and Silver

Other Recommended Materials and Tools:

- Clover Soft Touch hooks and Clover tip embroidery needles
- Alene's Tacky Glue